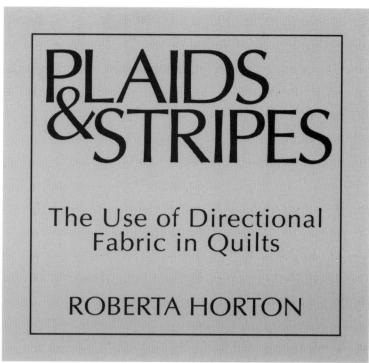

PLAIDS & STRIPES

The Use of Directional Fabric in Quilts

ROBERTA HORTON

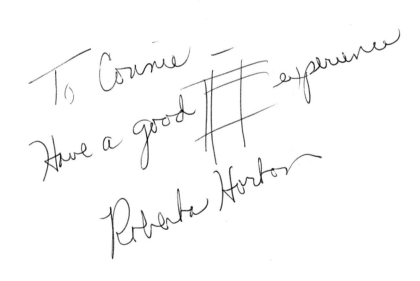

To Connie —
Have a good ⌗ ⌗ experience

Roberta Horton

C&T PUBLISHING

Cover:
"38 Lines Zigzag"
65" x 81"
Roberta Horton

Quotation from *A People and Their Quilts* used
with the permission of John Rice Irwin.

Photography by Sharon Risedorph
San Francisco, California

Editing by Sayre Van Young
Berkeley, California

Design/Production Coordination by Bobbi Sloan Design
Berkeley, California

Illustrations by Lisa Krieshok
Berkeley, California

Typesetting by Byron Brown/MACAW
Oakland, California

Published by C & T Publishing
P.O. Box 1456
Lafayette, CA 94549

IBSN: 0-914881-29-9

Library of Congress Catalog Card Number: 89-82564

Printed in Hong Kong

To Mary and our second fifty years of collaboration in life.

1929 El Dorado. 24" x 20".
Nancy Freeman, Alamo, CA, 1989.

CONTENTS

Color section appears after page 64.

INTRODUCTION

My first "plaid experience" was as a young, new sewer when I made a yellow plaid coat for my Terri Lee doll. I had enough savvy to match the plaids horizontally across the two front pieces (was it an accident?), but I didn't know enough, yet, to match the front and back pieces at the side seams. My handmade buttonholes and bias tape neck facing fell short of my present standards, but the coat was a fairly competent job, considering my tender age.

My next memorable "plaid experience" was as a college freshman. In the intervening years, I had learned the art, and necessity, of matching plaids, so the side seams in my wool plaid skirt passed muster. The professor wasn't overly impressed with the garment, however, since I had scorched the fabric during the final press job.

When I made the switch from being a sewer of clothes to a maker of quilts, I carried a lot of the baggage from my former life into my new interest. I had by this time taught home economics for five years, and I've always maintained that there is no one as uptight and rigid about sewing as a home ec teacher. Quilting proved a wonderful obsession, and ultimately caused me to discard a lot of the truths and absolutes I knew about fabric use. One of the biggest surprises concerned the use of plaids and stripes.

In 1987, I was asked to design a collection of plaids and stripes by Fabric Sales Company of Seattle, Washington. I lacked a textile design background, but I had been a quiltmaker for seventeen years. And so my focus was to create plaids and stripes that would be fun to work with in quilts. My Lines Collection was inspired by some favorite fabrics found in old quilts, quilt blocks, and fabric fragments I had collected over the years. Homespun Heritage II was based on old homespun fabrics. My Mood Indigo Collection was inspired by antique Japanese fabrics that fascinated me.

The fabric is handwoven in Cannanore, India. What an opportunity to have the fabric made "the old fashioned way!" These photographs show some of the processes and steps necessary to make the yarn into yardage.

Many quilts featured in this book do have some of my fabrics in them, although that certainly isn't a requirement! You can begin your plaid and stripe collection at your own quilt or fabric store. If my fabrics aren't available locally and you would like to use them, they can be mail-ordered. Check the Appendix under "Sources."

As always, I encourage you to start at the beginning and proceed chapter by chapter through to the end. At least read Chapter 1 before tackling a particular subject. Quilt categories covered here are traditional, utility, Log Cabins, African-American, appliqué, and contemporary. I've included some sewing hints I hope you will find useful, as well as some special tricks I have learned over the years. The last two chapters, "Backings, Bindings, and Labels," and "Quilting," deal with what happens after you finish the quilt top, the 50% of making a quilt we often forget about in the great scheme of things.

Photo I.1.   After the yarns have been sorted by weight and boiled to decrease shrinkage, the yarn is dyed by hand to match the colors I have submitted. (Photo by Sunit Gupta.)

Photo I.2.   The yarn is then dried in the courtyard. Some of the yarns look streaked; they've been stenciled with additional dye to create special effects (called ikat or twisted thread) when the thread is woven. (Photo by Sunit Gupta.)

Photo I.3.   The warp is prepared before it can be joined on the loom. (Photo by Sunit Gupta.)

Photo I.4. A winder woman prepares small bobbins of yarn. (Photo by Sunit Gupta.)

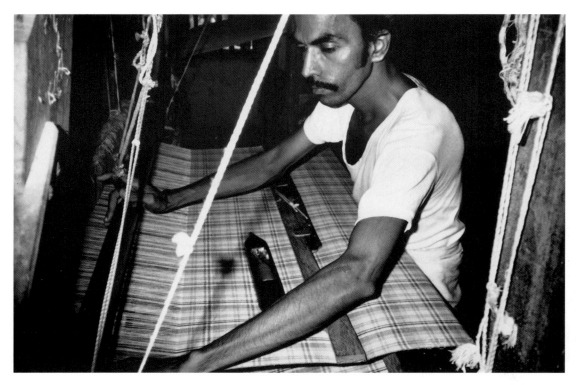

Photo I.5. Fabric from the Lines Collection being woven. (Photo by Sunit Gupta.)

1

UNDERSTANDING THE FABRIC

Plaids and stripes, more than any other fabric designs, have mercurial personalities, that is, they are capable of doing different things in a quilt. Some, dowdy and plain, are good for filler or a background area to which you don't want to call attention. They are noncontroversial. Others are real showoffs, commanding attention. There's no way to ignore them. Some are calm, others are busy. In fact, calm and busy are two of the most important concepts to understand in a successful use of plaids and stripes. Not everyone can be a Hollywood star; a supporting cast is also necessary for a good movie.

As with other fabrics, value, scale, color, and mood are important to consider. Plaids and stripes, however, present some unique considerations: grain, weave, and the all-important busy-calm difference. To better understand these similarities and differences, let's more thoroughly examine plaids and stripes.

DEFINITION

Plaids and stripes are fabrics which feature lines as the decorative element. Plaids are composed of bars or stripes of various colors and widths that cross at right angles. Stripes have the lines going only in one direction. To simplify things throughout this discussion, I use the term "directionals" for fabrics which feature lines (Photo 1.1).

Stripes

Plaids

Photo 1.1.

In woven directionals, the pattern is created through the change in color of the threads which create the fabric. The grainline is represented by any thread which goes horizontally or vertically across the fabric, making it unnecessary to have a selvage to determine whether the grainline is straight or not. If a woven directional appears to be off-grain, merely pulling on it will realign the grainline. (This is best done after washing because the washing itself may realign all the threads.) The fabric, on-grain when woven, sometimes becomes askew during the processing and wrapping on the bolts. See Figure 1.1.

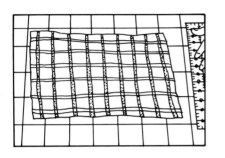 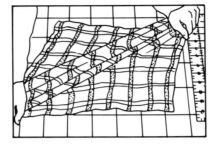 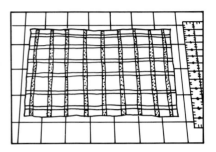

Off-grain   Pull on Opposite Corners   On-grain

Figure 1.1.   Straightening the Grain

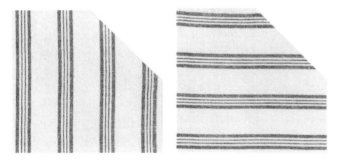

Photo 1.2.   Flipping over a woven stripe changes the direction of the lines.

Woven directionals are reversible because the thread itself is dyed, not the finished fabric. Sometimes this feature proves particularly handy in quilt composition; flipping over a stripe changes the direction of the lines (Photo 1.2). Flipping a plaid can change the density distribution, coloration arrangement, or even the composition (Photo 1.3).

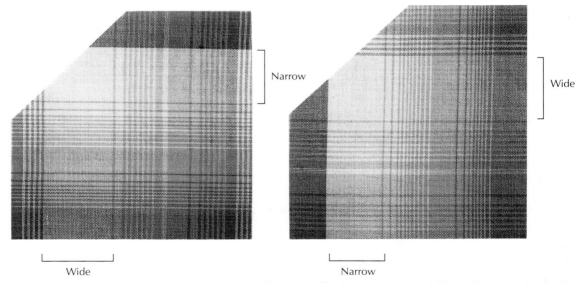

Photo 1.3.   Flipping over a woven plaid can change density distribution, coloration arrangement, or composition.

Printed directionals must be handled differently. The plaid or stripe pattern is printed onto already-woven fabric. The visual grainline of the design may not truly match the actual woven grainline. Then the quilter has the dilemma of which to follow. In most cases, I advocate going by the visual grainline. Contrary to popular opinion, having a piece here or there off-grain doesn't make a quilt fall apart.

Printed directionals aren't reversible; instead they have a muted version on the back. Sometimes, a paler or softer version or a lighter value is exactly what's needed in a project. I prefer to think positively—I call the wrong side, the other side. See Photo 1.4.

Photo 1.4. Printed directionals are muted on the back.

Some directionals are printed diagonally. This avoids the problem of the visual and actual grainlines not matching, which is often the case in printed directionals close to the selvage. However, the fabric reads even busier than if the same pattern were straight (Photo 1.5).

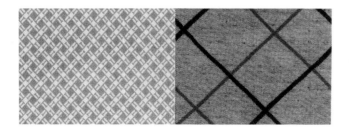

Photo 1.5. Printed Diagonal Plaids

The one category of striped fabric not covered here is the printed floral stripe. When combined with directionals which only feature lines in the design, floral stripes read and behave like printed calico fabric. They don't possess the clear graphic qualities of true directionals (Photo 1.6).

Photo 1.6. Printed floral stripes read like calico.

GRAIN

Many quiltmakers have a home sewing background. I can still remember being taught in an early home economics class to place the tissue paper pattern on the fabric so the big black arrow was positioned parallel to the selvage. We first pinned one end of the arrow to the yardage and measured the distance to the fabric edge. Then we pivoted the other end of the arrow until that measurement was equal to the first. Now our garment would hang correctly on the body. This made a big impression on me; I sometimes think many of us have an indelible arrow printed on our brain, demanding that we always have that grainline straight.

It's true, from a sewer's point of view, that the grainline should ideally be placed parallel to an edge on one, if not two, of the sides to cut down on stretching of the pieces through handling and sewing. When having to deal with bias edges (those cut markedly off-grain), try to join a bias with a straight edge for strength. Sides on the perimeter of the block, or of the

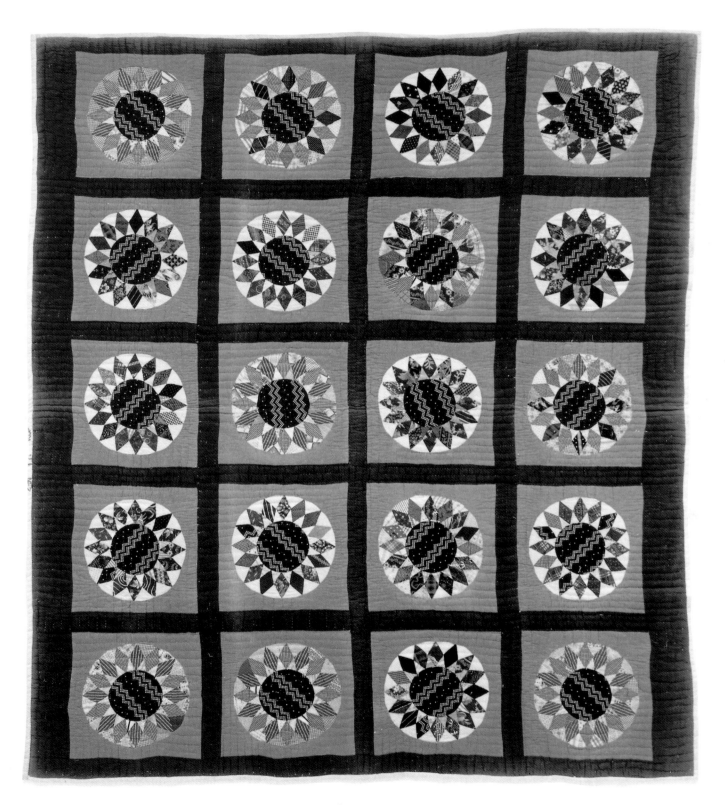

Photo 1.7.   Sunburst. 66" x 78". Georgia. A real country scrap quilt, with some of the fabric pre-Civil War. Sashing and background are hand-dyed. Collection of the author.

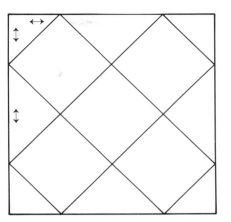

Figure 1.2.   Perimeter Edges On-grain

Photo 1.7A.   *Sunburst* (detail).

Photo 1.7B.   *Sunburst* (detail).

quilt top itself, should be on-grain to prevent stretching. Remember, though, this is the ideal. See Figure 1.2.

Plaids and stripes show their grainline through the actual threads of the pattern. I think many quiltmakers have chosen not to work with directional fabrics because even the slightest error in accuracy is there for all the world to see. Rare is the quiltmaking teacher who will suggest that her beginning students include a directional in their fabric selection. I know I didn't. I thought directionals should be saved for more advanced projects and skills. How wrong I was!

This obsession with accuracy, based on our clothing sewing skills, has robbed a whole generation of quiltmakers of the fun of working with plaids and stripes. Earlier quiltmakers weren't so fussy. Old quilts abound with directional fabrics, both on- and off-grain. They added a lot to the character and charm of those quilts. Sometimes I feel it's an example of knowing too much for our own good. See Photo 1.7.

Photo 1.8.   Twilight Houses (detail). 40½" x 49". Barbara Dallas, Moraga, CA, 1989. Casually off-grain use of plaid.

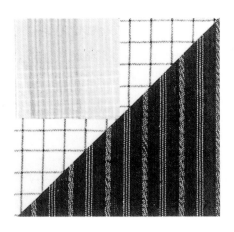

On-grain

Casually Off-grain

Photo 1.9.

So I'm going to advocate a new term. It's called "casually off-grain" and means that the grainline may be slightly askew. The hardest part about this concept is remembering that it's all right when it happens naturally. It's the result of reality intruding into the life of a quiltmaker. The house block from Barbara Dallas' "Twilight Houses" (Photo 1.8) is a good example of this. There's a spontaneous feeling to her house; it doesn't feel controlled or overworked. I think the block is much more enjoyable than if the house were more carefully cut out, with each piece lined up exactly.

Consider what happens visually when we play with the lines of a directional fabric. On-grain alignment, with the lines parallel or perpendicular to the edge of a template shape, stops the eye. That same fabric placed off-grain suggests movement. Sometimes we need an area of restfullness or calmness within a quilt and sometimes we need to spice up a particular area. Both of these can be accomplished merely by changing the grainline of the directional fabrics.

Look at Photo 1.9. In the first block, all grainlines are perfectly controlled. In the second block, some of the directionals are perfectly lined up with the seam edges of the triangles while others are not so perfectly aligned. This version has much more life than the first rendition. And we know which took the longest to cut out!

Personally, I stack cut whenever I can, trying to do four layers of fabric at a time. Why waste all the time and effort of cutting out each piece individually? I use my rotary cutter and a graph paper or plastic template which includes the seam allowance. Try this method:

1. Position the template on the fabric. If you're right-handed, position a ruler on the left-hand side of the template. (Left-handed quilters will position the ruler on the right-hand side.) See Figure 1.3.

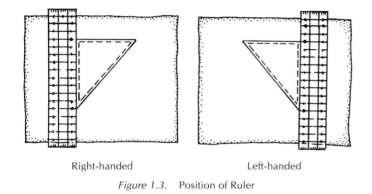

Right-handed   Left-handed

Figure 1.3.   Position of Ruler

2. Mentally note the measurement on the ruler where the template shape begins and ends. Remove the template. Make a cut beginning slightly before the measurement and ending slightly beyond the second measurement. Use the side of the tip of your fourth finger to keep the ruler from moving (Figure 1.4).

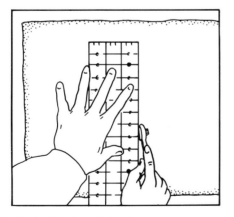

Figure 1.4.   Getting Ready to Make Cut

3. Reposition the template back on the fabric, next to the first cut. Rotate the fabric so that the next area to be cut is again on the left-hand side (Figure 1.5).
4. Repeat until all sides have been cut.

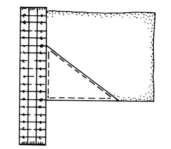

Figure 1.5.   Reposition template and rotate fabric for next cut.

When I stack-cut multiple layers of directionals, I'm not overly concerned that each piece come out exactly on-grain. In fact, I hope for slight variations—I know that if every piece is cut perfectly on-grain, the result will be visually boring and lifeless.

The concept of "casually off-grain" also opens up the potential for using directional fabrics when making "generated quilts." These speed or quick quilts have the advantage of being fast to make because one pattern block and one fabric choice are used consistently throughout the quilt. Once the fabric is selected, it can then be mass cut for efficiency. Plaids and stripes are not normally chosen for generated quilts because all the resulting pieces have the potential to be slightly, or even radically, different design-wise from each other depending on the directional fabric used. Uniformity is what is desirable, though this sameness is what often makes these quilts boring to live with. There are no surprises. I suggest there's room for rethinking fabric selection for generated quilts. Plaids and stripes offer the potential for some life and vitality!

Finally, grainline can give either a static feeling or a sense of movement, just by the degree to which it is placed on- or off-grain. Whether you want to emphasize movement or decrease it, remember you can exert control and create excitement in your work simply by varying the grainline.

WEAVES AND PATTERNS

It's not necessary for a quiltmaker to be able to correctly identify or label a directional before being able to use it. I present the following information more as a way to help train your eye so you can be on the lookout for variety, both in selecting and in usage. Don't feel you have to know every theoretical detail about weaves and patterns before you begin.

Stripes are the easiest to understand because the design bars only go in one direction. Even stripes feature bars that are equal in width all the way across the fabric; uneven stripes feature a variety of widths in the bars. Even stripes are generally calmer while uneven stripes present a busier facade to the world. Multicolor uneven stripes are busier than uneven stripes composed of only two colors (Photo 1.10). Another version is graduated stripes. Within a sequence, the bars start out narrow and get progressively wider. Numerous sequences are repeated across the fabric. This type sometimes gives a wonderful blurred feeling when viewed from afar (Photo 1.11).

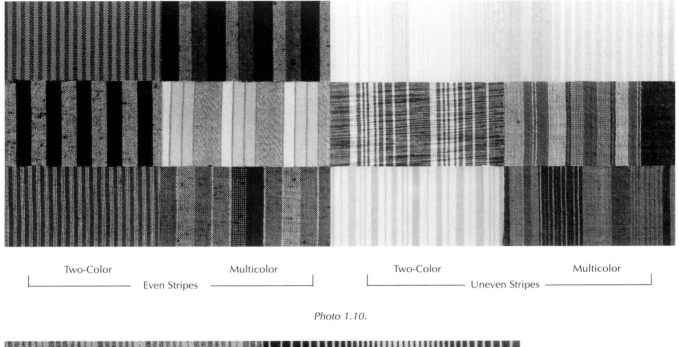

Two-Color	Multicolor	Two-Color	Multicolor
Even Stripes		Uneven Stripes	

Photo 1.10.

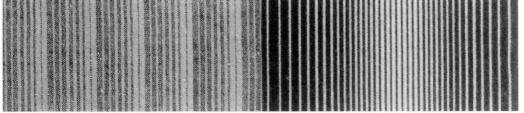

Photo 1.11.   Graduated Stripes

The simplest plaids have narrow lines running at right angles to each other. These windowpane plaids are the plainest and also the most easily used. Nancy Freeman has used two windowpane plaids in her appliqué composition "Spring Garden Fruit & Vegetables." Notice that the sidewalk plaid isn't perfectly on-grain (Photo 1.12).

Photo 1.12.
Spring Garden Fruit &
Vegetables. 30" x 22".
Nancy Freeman,
Alamo, CA, 1986.
(Photo by Nancy
Freeman.)

Most plaids are more complicated. The primary way to distinguish them is by whether they are even or uneven. I prefer the terms symmetrical or asymmetrical. Symmetrical plaids have a midpoint from which the design "mirror images" itself. True symmetrical plaids mirror image right and left from the midpoint as well as top and bottom from the midpoint. Some only mirror image from right to left. Asymmetrical plaids don't have this sameness of composition. There's no true center of the design (Photo 1.13).

From a quiltmaker's viewpoint, all you need to know is that the symmetrical plaids tend to read calmer (or more boring) than the asymmetrical ones because there is less to see or understand visually. In most cases, quiltmakers don't have the constraints of garment construction, where symmetrical plaids are often preferred because of the amount of pattern matching involved. Many of the plaids made specifically for quilters are symmetrical; if you use these exclusively, your composition can become boring. Combining symmetrical with asymmetrical plaids makes for maximum interest.

Symmetrical Plaid   Asymmetrical Plaid

Photo 1.13.

Most plaids are laid out in a square box format although occasionally one will be elongated to a rectangle. This type offers a nice contrast to the more commonly found square. Remember, search for variety as opposed to sameness (Photo 1.14).

In ikat weaving, the yarn is first dyed with a design and then woven. The result is a change of color along the thread. The thread will sometimes look like it has disappeared because a section has blended into the dominant color of an area. This can give an intriguing blurred appearance. Other times the ikat thread appears as a small area or slub of different color. Ikats are visually interesting to look at and are a wonderful contrast to the solid color lines normally found in plaids and stripes (Photo 1.15).

Photo 1.14.
Elongated Plaid

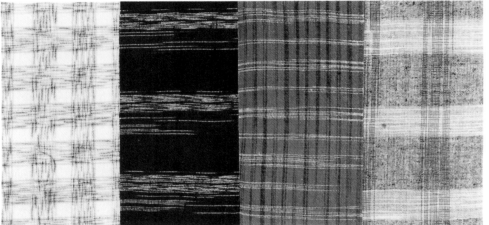

Photo 1.15.
Ikats

VALUE

Value—the degree of lightness or darkness of a fabric—is one of the most important aspects of quilt construction. It allows the viewer to differentiate between the separate pieces of a block, defines the block image or picture through contrast of light and dark, and assures the overall design impact of the quilt. The use of dark, medium, and light gives depth to a quilt because our eyes don't read dark and light on the same visual plane. Normally, light comes toward the viewer and dark recedes (although just the opposite can happen). Through a skillful use of value, we can make part of the quilt feel flat and another part dimensional. We can make one area blend into another, altering the image seen. Value, carefully used, can be even more effective than color!

So, when purchasing plaids and stripes for a fabric collection or for a specific project, think about buying examples of light *and* medium *and* dark. Everyone has a natural value thermostat that favors one of the values more than another, but it's imperative to have a good representation of all the values. (More medium directionals are available, probably because so many are designed for clothing.)

For me, light directionals are the hardest to find, and then even harder to make myself purchase. Consider the number of lights it took for me to make "Plaids on Hand" (Color Plate 9A). Several years ago, I probably wouldn't have had the necessary amount, but I've learned to collect a broad representation of different values and have accepted the challenge of using them. It helps to think of the lights as muslin replacements.

Plaids and stripes used as the background in a block give the quiltmaker additional opportunity to provide some visual interest. Study Photo 1.16. Think about the activity level of both the other fabrics used and of the finished block itself, and then select accordingly. The most visually boring light directionals often prove to be the most useful (Photo 1.17).

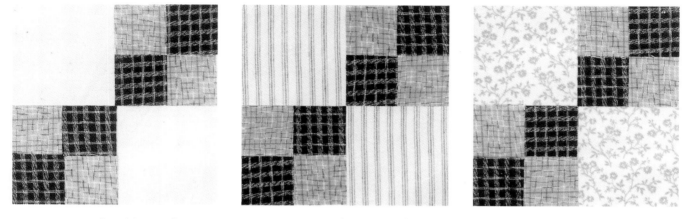

A. Muslin + Directionals

B. Directional + Directionals

C. Calico Print + Directionals

Photo 1.16.

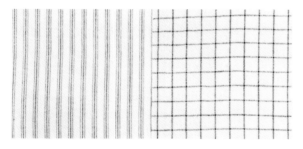

Photo 1.17.   Boring but Useful Light Directionals

An additional unique aspect of plaids and stripes, in relation to value, is what is happening within the pattern itself. Patterns with minimum value contrast read flatter than those with high value contrast. The more value contrast, the further away the pattern can be read as a directional. Plaids with complicated patterns and a marked value contrast between the threads of design and background often have a look I call "interior illumination." See Photo 1.18. These plaids, which often looks like boys' shirting, can be particularly beautiful and tend to show well from afar in a quilt. Care must be executed in their use, however. They are best rationed as too many interior illumination fabrics will cancel their specialness. Especially if surrounded with lower contrast fabrics, though, they really shine (Photo 1.19).

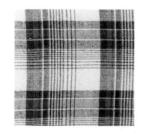

Photo 1.18.   Interior Illumination

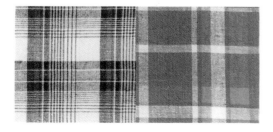

Interior Illumination + Busy Directional

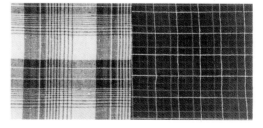

Interior Illumination + Calm Directional

Photo 1.19.

Photo 1.20.   Move window template around interior illumination fabric to discover possibilities.

When searching for the interior illumination effect, try using a triangle window template so you can see what a small section looks like as opposed to a whole hunk of yardage. Learning to see the potential of plaids and stripes is a visualization learning process, similar to what we all went through with small prints. Some of the fabrics which feature interior illumination may feel too garish or bold at first. Once you can identify the "look," you will find yourself buying this type in advance of specifically needing it. And once you've become familiar with it, you'll find it neither garish nor bold, but visually exciting and alive (Photo 1.20).

SCALE

Scale refers to the size of the pattern of the plaid or stripe. Variety in your fabric collection is important for visual interest in the resulting quilts. In general, the smaller-scale directionals tend to read as a solid from afar which makes them the safest to use. Large-scale directionals can be seen as a plaid or stripe from a distance and tend to make more of an impact in the composition. Small-scale directionals tend to read as calm, whereas larger-scale ones are more likely to feel busy (Photo 1.21).

Consider how you can use this variety of scale within a quilt. Initially you see the quilt from a distance, perhaps from across the room at a quilt show. Some of the directionals should read as plaids and stripes in contrast to the solids and prints in the piece. As you move closer, more of the fabric should read as a directional; some pieces that you at first took to be a solid, will now read as a directional. That's the joy of seeing the quilt up close. As a quiltmaker, you want more and more information to gradually unfold as the viewer approaches the quilt. That's the reward for walking over to see it. As a viewer, you too want that reward of unfolding, everchanging visual excitement (Photo 1.22 A–C on pages 22 and 23).

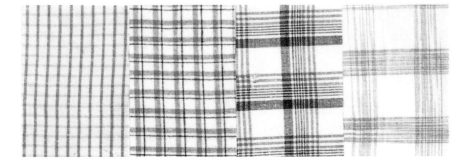

Photo 1.21.
Small-scale to Large-scale
Calm to Busy

Small-scale + Small-scale   Large-scale + Large-scale   Small-scale + Large-scale

Photo 1.23.

Particularly when working with individual block compositions, consider the scale of the directionals as you combine them with other directionals or prints. Most often, small would be put with larger as opposed to small plus small, or large plus large. This isn't an ironclad rule because you need to know what personality is required of that block. If you need some activity in a boring area, for example, you might make both fabrics large-scale. Or conversely, if you really need to quiet down an area, then both choices should be small-scale patterns (Photo 1.23).

Look at Elaine Anderson's "Square Within a Square" (Color Plate 14B). A large red-and-black plaid plays an important part in this quilt. In the interior of the quilt, the plaid acts as an area of stability in contrast to the diagonal lines of the nearby strip piecing. It also mimics the red-and-black checkerboard above it. Then it reappears in the border. Notice that the plaid is cut in such a way that the more muted area of weaving is used this time so that its effect is softer, almost blurred. This red-and-black plaid is both large-scale and high contrast.

NUMBER OF COLORS

The calmest directionals, with only two colors, are the easiest to use but can also become boring if used exclusively. Many of the plaids and stripes specifically printed for quilters are like this (Photo 1.24).

The addition of more colors can intensify the activity level of a plaid or stripe. Width of the bars and value contrast of the colors used within the design also factor into this busyness level, of course. The best bet is not to restrict yourself to only two-color directionals or only multicolor directionals, but to strike a balance. Think about the need for variety in advance so that as you purchase directionals for your collection, you'll get representatives of both.

MOOD

Many of the quilts featured in the Color Section project a feeling of antiquity or oldness, while others have a much more contemporary flair. This "ageness" is

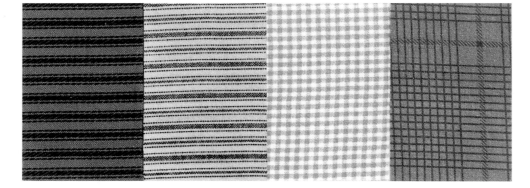

Photo 1.24.
Two-color Directionals

Photo 1.22A.   Devil's Claw. 77" x 85". 1900. Collection of
Bernice McCoy Stone. Quilt seen from afar.

Photo 1.22B.   Devil's Claw (detail). Quilt seen closer.

Photo 1.22C.   Devil's Claw (detail).
Quilt seen closer yet.

accomplished through pattern and fabric selection, color use, set, and border choice. One way to most dramatically see how mood and period can be created is to compare two quilts with the same pattern. Look at the bow ties in Color Plates 2A and 9A. The choice of the brighter and more varied colors plus the handling of the border make my "Plaids on Hand" feel more contemporary in mood; Elaine Anderson's "Grandfather's Tie Collection" feels like a wonderfully loved antique. Set and border choice are more fully explored in Chapter 8. Now, let's consider pattern selection and color use in setting the mood.

When thinking specifically about directional choices for mood setting, you'll find those that feature loud colors and a larger scale definitely feel more contemporary. Lights with an off-white to tan coloration look older than those with a pure white background. Don't fall into the trap, however, of thinking that all your background whites must match.

It's more visually exciting if there is some value variation within the quilt. Study Betty Kisbey's "Lines Pineapple Log Cabin" (Color Plate 11A), a beautiful example of this.

When in the quilt composing stage, remember to stand back from your design and analyze if the right mood is appearing. Particularly when creating a scrap-quilt look, it's important to be composing all your blocks at the same time. The directionals chosen for one block, by itself, might look fine but when considered in the whole composition, the directionals may not work and other choices may be necessary.

Notice how Charlene Phenney used a variety of whites and tans in her "Remembrance in Plaids" (Color Plate 4A). The quilt feels old even though she didn't restrict her choice in lights only to off-whites and tans. White brings life into a quilt!

Judy Mathieson has mixed moods in her "Plaid Compass Rose" (Photo 1.25) by combining plaids

Photo 1.25.   Plaid Compass Rose (unquilted top). 96" x 96". Judy Mathieson, Woodland Hills, CA, 1989. (Photo by Jack Mathieson.)

inspired by old fabrics with those with a more modern feel. Most quiltmakers wouldn't think of combining the traditional plaid with the ikat shown in Photo 1.26. But because the two fabrics are of similar scale, value, and color, they can be paired successfully, as seen in the finished block in Photo 1.27. Judy has used a large printed flower for the compass center and added other interesting large-scale prints around the outside edge.

Traditional Plaid   Ikat

Photo 1.26.

Photo 1.27.   Plaid Compass Rose (detail). 96" x 96". Judy Mathieson, Woodland Hills, CA, 1989. (Photo by Jack Mathieson.)

SUMMARY

Now you should be ready to try out some of this information about plaids and stripes in a project. The following chapters deal with different types of quilts and the use of directional fabrics in their composition. Suggestions relating to the finishing of the quilt are also included.

The following chart can serve as a quick reference to the calm-busy characteristics of plaids and stripes, as discussed throughout this chapter.

CALM	BUSY
on-grain	off-grain
symmetrical	asymmetrical
even	uneven
stripes	plaids
solid lines	ikat
low value contrast	high value contrast
flat reading	interior illumination
small	large
two color	multicolor

2

TRADITIONAL PIECED PATTERNS

PATTERN SELECTION

Plaids and stripes, by their very nature, make a strong design statement. To showcase this type of fabric, you don't have to work with intricate pieced patterns or undertake complicated gyrations in your quilt block arrangements. Sometimes, simpler is better.

This chapter features some simple pieced designs, most having only two or three template shapes. Patterns for making twelve of the designs can be found at the end of the chapter. I recommend trying a project where you work only with directionals to get a better handle on this type of fabric. Plaids and stripes combine well with prints and solids, but you will learn more, that is, experience more surprises and shocks, if you purposely restrict your fabric choice only to plaids and stripes.

Work with at least a 6" block so that the individual

template shapes are large enough to show off the fabric. Any fabric can be used in a quilt if you cut it small enough. The challenge, then, is to cut it large enough that it matters. If you have ever looked closely at an antique Log Cabin quilt, you've seen what I mean. From afar, all you really notice is the color and value and not the individual designs on the fabrics.

You need to know only two things to be able to draft any of these patterns. The first is to be able to recognize what grid format is used for the pattern; the second is to know how to change the finished size of the block. I'm including a description of drafting your own block right here in the text rather than relegating it to an appendix because I'm amazed at the number of quiltmakers I meet who don't know this information. If you're already familiar with this liberating information, skip ahead to the section on "Getting Started."

Two-Patch

Nine-Patch (Three-Patch)

Four-Patch

Five-Patch

Seven-Patch

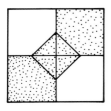

Bow Tie Block

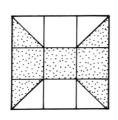

Spool Block

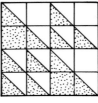

Flock Block

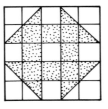

Monkey Wrench Block

Bear's Paw Block

Figure 2.1. Most Common Grids

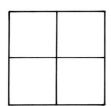

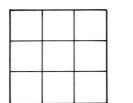

Drafting the Pattern

Drafting decisions aren't made arbitrarily; usually some logical and easily seen reference point acts as a guide. Most pieced patterns (at least enough to keep us amused for a long time) are based on a square divided into a given number of equal-size units. To establish the grid size, look for the tiniest unit and then see how many times you can divide it into one side. Figure 2.1 shows the most common grids with a pattern below each one made from that grid.

When making templates from this drafted pattern, it isn't essential to use all the lines of the original grid. Try to make each shape as big as possible, in essence erasing unnecessary lines (Figure 2.2). Don't make yourself more work than is necessary. This is particularly true when working with directionals, where a chopped-up look can all too easily be created.

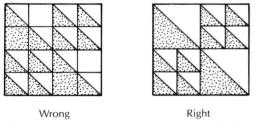

Wrong   Right

Figure 2.2.   Make each shape as big as possible.94

Another group of blocks can be created by using an X-and-cross format. See Figure 2.3. To begin, draw a square. Divide the square into fourths with a cross; make an X in the square by drawing lines that connect

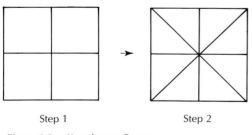

Step 1   Step 2

Figure 2.3.   X-and-cross Format

opposite corners. By connecting midpoints on the X segments with quarter points on the sides (Figure 2.4), you can create the "End of the Day" pattern used by Barb Kolby (Color Plate 3A).

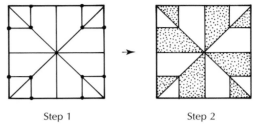

Step 1   Step 2

Figure 2.4.   End of the Day Block

Now, draw another square. This time only draw the X. Now connect midpoints of the segments of the X with the midpoints of the sides of the square (Figure 2.5). Again, don't necessarily use all the lines in the original drawing. Kathy Ezell used this pattern called "Windmills in Time" for her quilt (Color Plate 3C).

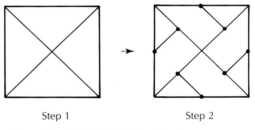

Step 1   Step 2

Figure 2.5.   Windmills in Time Block

Sometimes a little detective work is necessary to find the key to how a particular block was created. Part of the drafting of "Pinwheel" by Mata Rolston in Color Plate 7B is easily seen, but part is far less obvious. Start with the X-and-cross format to form a block like that in Figure 2.3. Divide the remaining large triangles into a smaller triangle and a trapezoid (a four-sided figure with only two sides parallel). Since it's a right-angle isosceles triangle (the two short sides are equal), it could be almost any size. The trapezoid is merely formed by the leftover space. The bigger the isosceles triangle, the skinnier the trapezoid. All versions are merely variations. Experiment until you find the proportions you like (Figure 2.6).

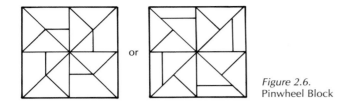

Figure 2.6.
Pinwheel Block

Or to save work (the goal of most quiltmakers), why not make the triangle the same size as the small triangle you already have? The version on the right in Figure 2.6 is the one used for Mata's quilt. Make a small triangle template (without any seam allowance) and place it in the large triangle, this time aligning the short leg on the cross. In its original position, the long leg is on the cross. Then there are only two templates rather than three for the block. You've gained more flexibility as to where you can insert the fabrics. And each fabric triangle cut will work in one-third more places.

"Plaid Lattice" by Rebecca Rohrkaste (Color Plate 8A), which is actually an Arabic Lattice pattern, appears quite tricky until a closer look reveals the triangles are created by drawing a line from a corner to the center of the opposite side. After this is done from each corner, the unnecessary part of each line is erased. The center square is divided into a four-patch and the design is finished. The squares in the set of these blocks also used the midpoint of a side to determine their size (Figure 2.7).

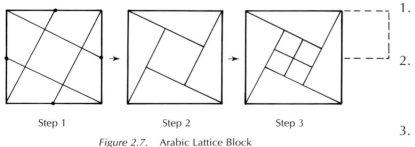

Step 1   Step 2   Step 3

Figure 2.7.   Arabic Lattice Block

Changing the Size of the Block

A quiltmaker really needs to know how to draft the desired block in various sizes. Many of us are locked into working only with patterns for which we have the templates. Or, if we draft the pattern ourselves, we only feel confident working with graph paper which often forces us into working in certain size increments because we want the lines of our block to correspond to the lines on the graph paper. For example, if a design has a grid of four, we can only execute it in a four-inch size, or eight inches, or twelve inches, and so on. Or, if we're really brave, perhaps we'll attempt a six- or ten-inch block, because those measurements are midway between.

Sometimes, though, a slightly smaller or larger version would do our pattern and fabric choice better justice. Use the following method to make any size block (see Figure 2.8):

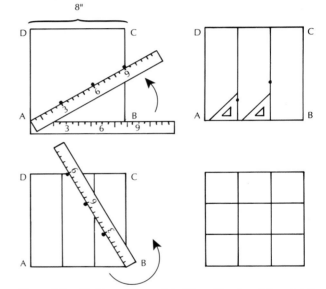

Figure 2.8.   Division of Space into Given Number of Equal Units

1. Use a ruler and a right-angle to draw a square the desired finished size on plain paper. Label the corners A B C D.
2. Using a ruler as a reference, identify the next number past the length of one side of your square that the grid number will divide into evenly. Let's call that number M (for magic).
3. Position the left-hand end of the ruler (zero) in the bottom left-hand corner (A). Using A as a pivot point, move the ruler up the opposite side (B-C) of the square until it intersects M, your magic number.
4. Divide M by the grid number. Using the resulting number, mark dots along the ruler at these evenly divided intervals.
5. Position a right-angle so that one side is on the bottom line (A-B) and the adjacent side touches a dot. Now draw a perpendicular

line that connects A-B to C-D. Do this for each interval dot. The square is now divided into equal intervals going in one direction.

6. Turn the paper one quarter turn, making B-C the bottom line. Repeat Steps 3 through 5 to get your second set of lines. You now have the necessary grid upon which to fill in your pattern.

Getting Started

For the simple blocks in this chapter, I suggest drawing your pattern in several sizes, not smaller than 6" and probably not larger than 12". The size will partially be determined by the complexity of the pattern itself as well as the scale of the fabric being considered. Also take into account visual impact. Sometimes we work smaller or larger to set a mood for the piece. And lastly, consider the finished size of the project. Four-inch bow ties would probably look ridiculous on a king-size quilt!

Place several different size drawings of the block, plus your proposed fabric, in front of you. You should be able to easily tell if one version feels too small or too big. Eliminate that choice. Check how much of the fabric would show in the various template shapes. You can usually tell what you don't like or what doesn't work right away. It's often harder to tell what you do like or what's "right." Sometimes a third or fourth size version is necessary. Using this process of comparison and elimination makes the selection easier. I sometimes end up with a choice quite different from the one that at first felt "right."

Once the size of the finished block is decided, and your design is drawn accurately, the next step is to make templates for each individual shape in the pattern. At this point, the ¼" seam allowance is added to all sides of each shape. I mark on each template both the number of pieces that need to be cut for one block and the correct value information (Figure 2.9), remem-

bering that in a scrap quilt this information doesn't always stay the same.

FABRIC CHOICE: COLOR AND VALUE

This is, of course, the fun part. Remember, using a lot of plaids and stripes can tend to create a busy effect, so manipulate the fabric and color choices to calm things down. I'm assuming you will want to work with a scrap approach so you can experiment with more combinations.

When you select the pattern, the first step is to decide how you will use value, that is, dark, medium, and light, within the block. The pattern should initially clearly be visible to add stability to the piece. As the quilt progresses, you might purposely blur or fade out an area. Some patterns can be used in several variations; see Mata Rolston's "Pinwheel" (Color Plate 7B and Figure 2.10). Think of one version as the major

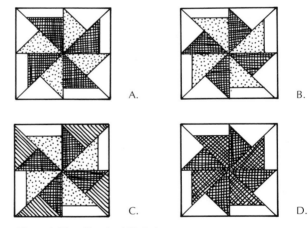

Figure 2.10.   Pinwheel Variations

one, and the others as the minor ones. This would be a less controlled choice than having variations positioned alternately in a checkerboard fashion. I find it helpful to tack up a small drawing of my block, with the values indicated, on my design wall next to where I'm composing (Figure 2.11).

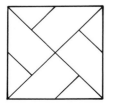

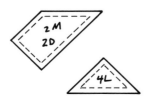

Figure 2.9.   Marking of Templates

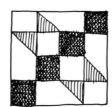

Figure 2.11.   Value Information Indicated

Color selection—and how you use colors—is also very important in a quilt featuring directionals. Sometimes it helps to limit the number of colors. The more colors, the more busy the quilt may appear. There are exceptions, of course. My "Plaids on Hand" (Color Plate 9A) is a polychromatic, or rainbow, color scheme which often can be busy when the colors are used randomly. In this quilt, though, the colors are controlled by restricting them to certain areas.

In general, use as few pieces of fabric within an individual block as possible. That is, repeat the same fabric in the same shape/position. Don't be afraid of making the block boring. Remember, it will be put with other blocks and will not be seen alone by itself. If each individual block reads busy, think how frenetic the whole quilt will be (Photo 2.1).

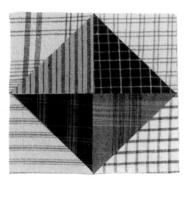

Many directionals used within the block.

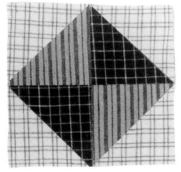

Minimum number of directionals used within the block.

Photo 2.1.

To give a scrap feeling, your next block should be composed of a new set of fabrics. Keep in mind some of the guidelines mentioned in Chapter 1 about effectively combining fabrics. The end result will be a lot of fabrics, but they will be clustered to give some stability. Don't be tempted to critique the results until at least four blocks are composed. A combination that might appear garish at first may seem okay with the other blocks surrounding it. Working on four blocks simultaneously also provides numerous places to try out your color choices (Photo 2.2).

Photo 2.2.   Flock of Geese (detail). 57" x 73 ½". Nancy Mahoney, Seattle, WA, 1989.

As the quilt progresses, you may find yourself repeating a fabric. That's all right—the definition of a scrap quilt merely states that the fabric isn't used consistently throughout <u>all</u> the blocks. Sometimes a block will be cloned with the fabrics in the same positions as in their first appearance. This can be calming. Or, if more variety is needed, the fabrics might be reassembled in a new way. Sometimes the outstanding or eye-catching block needs to be repeated and sometimes a homely or boring block, though a noncontroversial filler, needs to be repeated.

As you continue to compose, stand back and look at what you're doing. A reducing glass helps because it shows a smaller version of the project with the value contrasts and similarities accentuated. Look at the games played in Joyce Miller's "Stars in Stripes" (Color Plate 7A). A star is discernable in the upper right-hand corner, with illusions of one in the bottom left-hand corner. There's also a hole near the bottom right where the lighter value triangles surround the nine-patch. Then there's also the illusion that a three-by-four block nine-patch quilt is floating diagonally across the quilt from the bottom right to the left border, except that one of the blocks is missing at the juncture with the border...

SPEED CUTTING vs. TRADITIONAL CUTTING

Whenever possible, I use shortcuts to speed up my quiltmaking; one such is using a rotary cutter. If I had discovered that method years ago, I would have many more quilts to share. Sometimes in the quest for speed, however, we sacrifice the look of the quilt. Though I use speed techniques, I'd rather no one, looking at my finished product, could tell. Two telltale signs of overuse of shortcuts: the same two fabrics always paired in half-a-square triangles, and the addition rather than the elimination of seams within the block. Avoiding this second sign is especially important when working with the lines of directional fabrics.

For example, a sailboat block can be cut and sewn in several ways. Compare the two methods—traditional and shortcut—for "ease" of viewing in the following areas (Figure 2.12):

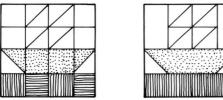

Shortcut	Traditional

Figure 2.12.   Sailboat Block

1. *Sails:* I definitely would use the fast method for making half-of-a-square triangles for the sails if I were going to use that set of fabrics over and over again (see "Techniques" in the Appendix for details). However, in a scrap quilt, I probably wouldn't use the fast way for two reasons. First, each combination of two fabrics would probably only be used in one block, making it not worth the bother. Secondly, I want the freedom to experiment and change those two fabrics in the half-of-a-square triangles as I compose the quilt on

the wall. So, I would probably cut the triangles as I needed them and then later sew them traditionally.

2. *Sailboat body:* I would prefer to have the sailboat body all one piece of fabric for continuity (as in Photo 2.3).

Photo 2.3.   *Fabric Sails* (detail). 63" x 40". Paula Fluder, Puyallup, WA, 1989.

3. *Sky:* Having the sky area a rectangle rather than two squares keeps it in the background. The additional seam would more likely call too much attention to that area.

4. *Water:* The water could be done either way. If I wanted a smooth sea, I would cut a rectangle, but if I wanted the sea to appear choppy, I would use four squares. Or I would use the rectangle, but cut it off-grain.

Sometimes a newer method can make the sewing easier. For example, there are two ways to cut and sew a bow tie. The traditional approach uses two templates: a five-sided shape for both the bow tie and the background, and the square that forms the knot. When joining the shapes, sewing can only be done to the intersection of these seam lines at the corners and not through the seam allowances. This requires marking the intersection point and then stopping sewing at that point (Figure 2.13).

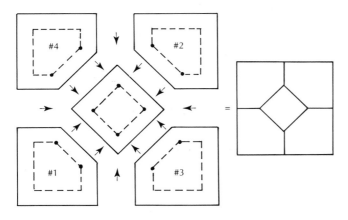

Figure 2.13. Traditional Sewing Method

(Quiltmakers who use a zigzag machine often complain about the difficulty in seeing where to stop stitching when using this technique. The wide presser foot blocks their vision. There is a special presser foot called a Little Foot which is ¼" wide and also has lines on it to show when you are ¼" away from an intersection. The Little Foot fits most standard short shank machines, including a Bernina, which requires an adapter. Buy one at your local quilt or fabric store or consult "Sources" in the Appendix.)

An easier way to sew a bow tie requires that when drafting the block, you divide the knot square into four triangles by drawing an X. You'll need two template shapes, the five-sided shape and a triangle. A triangle is sewn to the five-sided shape, thus turning it into a square. Now it's merely a matter of sewing four squares together to form the bow tie, mechanically a far easier task (Figure 2.14).

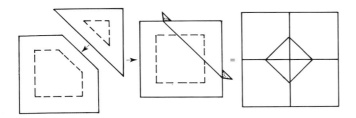

Figure 2.14. Easier Sewing Method

When comparing the final results, however, you'll find a marked difference in appearance. In the second method, the added seams in the knot mean quite a bit of visual confusion. Calico prints with their tiny busyness would probably disguise the seams but directional fabrics emphasize the seams, because it's likely the lines haven't rejoined "correctly." Since plaids can tend to be busy, especially if both the bow tie and the background are directionals, I would veto this simpler method of sewing which results in more seams and more misaligned design lines (Photo 2.4).

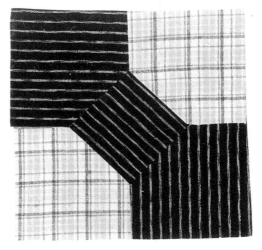

Knot = One Square = CALM

Photo 2.4.

Knot = Four Triangles = BUSY

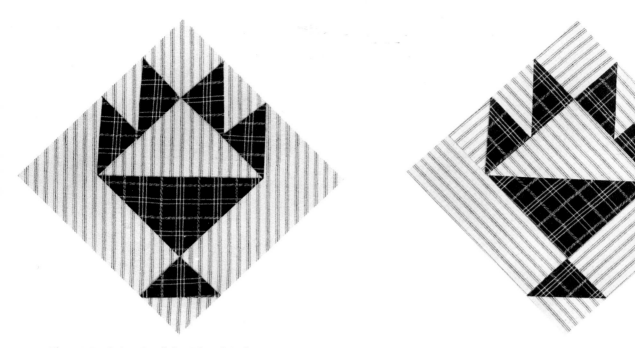

Photo 2.5.   Stripes Parallel to Edge of Quilt

Photo 2.6.   Stripes Parallel to Edge of Block

GRAINLINE

Remember when cutting your fabric that directionals placed parallel to an edge are calming and stop the eye, while those placed askew tend to give movement. The concept of "casually off-grain" adds just enough life to a piece to make it more interesting than if everything is perfectly controlled.

Do some experimenting to figure out the most satisfactory arrangement of the grain each time you start a new block. As you compose on your design wall, try various configurations. Just turning a square a quarter-turn or flipping a triangle over often changes the visual grain. Sometimes both ways look good, so you might have most of the blocks done one way, with just a few in the alternate arrangement.

Watching students compose with stripes for the first time, I have observed that some of them think that for their composition to be "right," they must exert absolute control over their directional fabrics. This is most obvious when they work with the finished blocks on point rather than parallel to the edge of the quilt. Instead of having the stripes (grain) line up with the template edge, they position the stripes so they will be parallel to the edge of the quilt (Photo 2.5), in effect actually cutting their shapes on the bias. This tight

control robs the block of its potential life as well as making it harder to sew. Follow common sense and don't be so manipulative. Let things happen more naturally (Photo 2.6).

PATCHING

If you compare antique quilts with those made today, one noticeable difference is the likely presence of some patching within the individual shapes of the pieced blocks in the antique quilts. When fabric was scarce, quiltmakers tended to be more frugal by using every small scrap of fabric possible. This "collaging" of fabric added a lot to the charm and spunk of these old quilts. Though these early quilters probably weren't patching for design reasons, why can't we?

Directional fabrics prove perfect for use in patching because when misaligned they will really show, rewarding your effort. By constrast, small prints used in a patch job only allow the seam to show with the closest scrutiny. Here are two ways to go about an on-purpose patch job.

Method I (Figure 2.15)

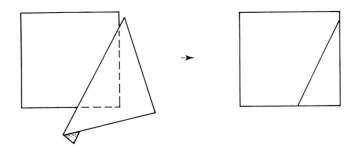

Figure 2.15. Patching (Method I)

1. Cut the potential patch larger than necessary; iron under the seam allowance on the edge to be sewn.
2. Manipulate the patch until a pleasing composition is achieved. Directionals will look the most exciting when misaligned.
3. Flip back the patch to expose the seam allowance. Sew along the crease. Then flip the patch back to the right side. Trim away any excess on the patch and underneath the patched area.

Method II (Figure 2.16)

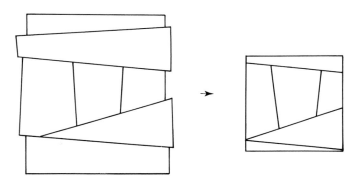

Figure 2.16. Patching (Method II)

1. Join together fabric strips of various widths. Make sure that the directionals are offset. The resulting fabric needs to be larger than the template shape.
2. Cut the desired shape from the patched fabric.

Patching can be done with matching fabric, as in Photo 2.7, or with contrasting fabric, as in Photo 2.8. Experiment, or in other words, have fun and play.

Photo 2.7.   Homespun Diamond in a Square (detail). 71" x 61". Roberta Horton, Berkeley, CA, 1985. Patch made with matching fabric.

Photo 2.8.   38 Lines Zigzag (detail). 65" x 81". Roberta Horton, Berkeley, CA, 1988. Patch made with contrasting fabric.

RENEGADE COLOR

When working with a limited number of colors, as is often the case when making a quilt with only plaid and stripe fabrics, it is often necessary to go beyond the initial color choice. In reality, the original combination may prove too safe and boring. Though sometimes this need gets downright desperate, it's probably easier to have a quilt be boring colorwise and then spice it up with a few changes or additions than to have it out of control from the beginning.

A "renegade" color can come to the rescue. I define a renegade as an accent color or a color that doesn't, seemingly, "belong." Renegade colors are loud and bright and tend to be red, orange, yellow, and turquoise. Quilters are often reluctant to use these "garish" colors. However, all renegades probably won't be used together in one quilt; in fact, not all quilts even need a renegade, though often a dash of renegade color makes a surprising difference. (Relax—the other, duller fabrics within the quilt tend to tone down renegades from how they appear as yardage.)

A renegade color should be repeated since a single use is far too eye-catching. Careful placement of the renegade color helps move the viewer's eye through the quilt. The uninitiated might not even be aware a renegade color has been used in a finished quilt because it looks like it belongs. If you had seen the quilt in progress, the need would have been apparent. In the finished quilt, though, the renegade looks natural. One way to tell if a color is serving as a renegade is to block out the suspected color with your finger when viewing the quilt and see how the quilt looks without it. If it looks boring and lifeless, you've found the renegade.

Kathy Ezell has used red as the renegade color in "Windmills in Time" (Color Plate 3C). The renegade block is even repeated in its entirety. This is often a good idea, especially when working with plaids and stripes, because the repetition calms down both the renegade's impact and the busyness of the directionals. The viewer's eye/mind can accept it more easily the second time

because the viewer doesn't have to reanalyze how it relates to its companions. One advantage of repetition is that you can make anything look like it belongs, just by repeating it enough. The question then becomes, "How often do I repeat the renegade color?" I used to think that unusual or unique things were best in odd numbers, like three or five. I have since discovered that two repetitions often works well, also. The completed size of the quilt and/or the degree of need are more important than any arbitrary number. Experiment.

Joyce Miller also used red as a renegade color in "Stars in Stripes" (Color Plate 7A). Red really stands out in three of the blocks, but each time, it's a slightly different red. Notice that one of the reds even dares to be brighter than the others. Gold, rust, and red all serve as renegades in my "38 Lines Zigzag" (Color Plate 1A). Though these colors don't stand out as much as the bright red renegade in "Stars in Stripes," think how dull the quilt would be without them.

Betty Mensinger's "Journey's End" (Color Plate 5B) used turquoise as the renegade color. The four turquoise triangles slash diagonally across the quilt. In some quilts, the orange or even the rust Betty used might be the renegade, but here they end up more as an extension of the browns used. As soon as the turquoise was added, it became the renegade. It comes closest to being the color that doesn't quite belong, yet the one that adds a special spark.

SUMMARY

Now, with these techniques for pattern drafting, fabric selection, and cutting, plus the additional insights on weave and color, you should be ready to go!

The following twelve designs are particularly good for working with directional fabrics because they are very simple and require few templates. Patterns are given in the size used in the actual quilts which appear in the Color Section. Most of the blocks are easy to sew. Arabic Lattice is included for those wishing more of a sewing challenge, and isn't recommended for beginners.

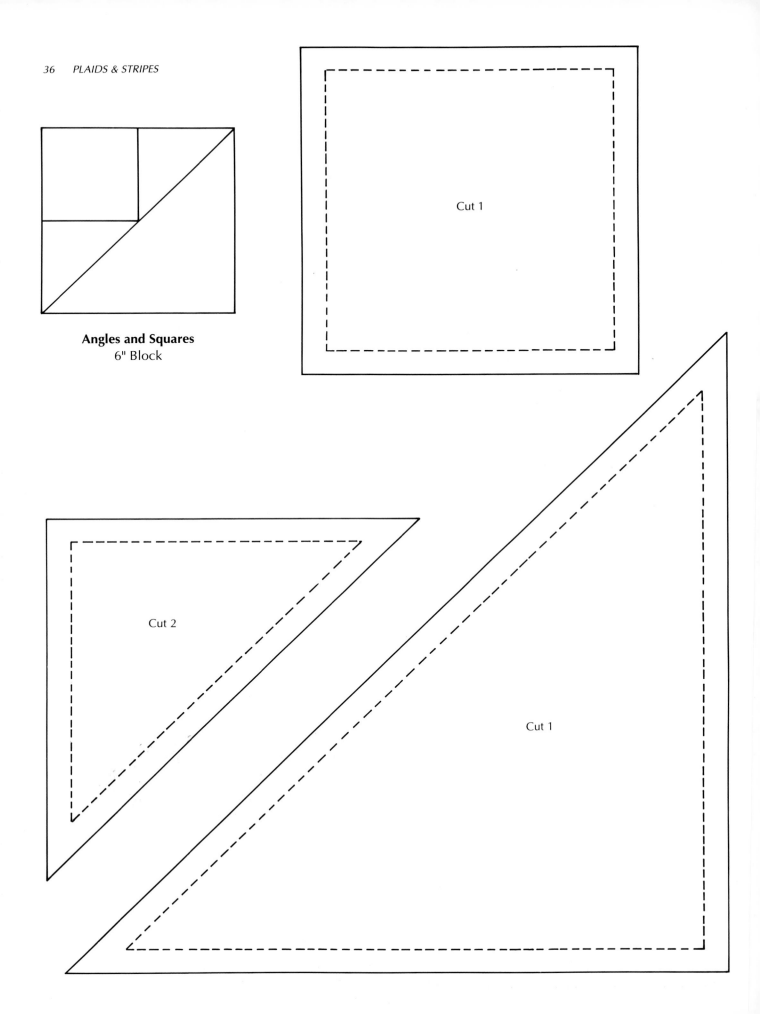

Angles and Squares
6" Block

Cut 1

Cut 2

Cut 1

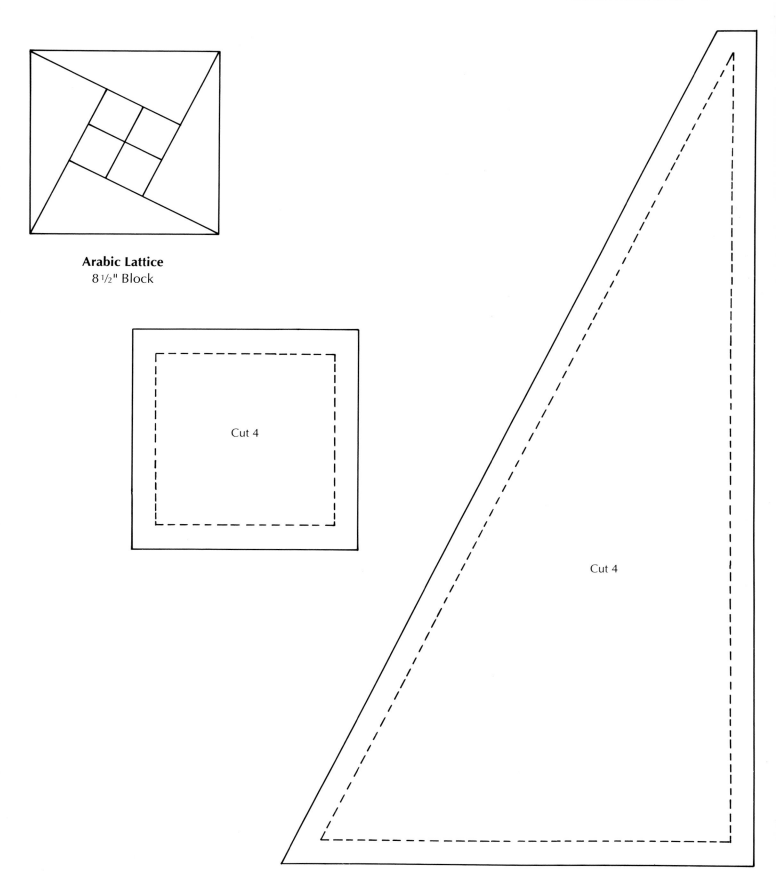

Arabic Lattice
8 1/2" Block

Cut 4

Cut 4

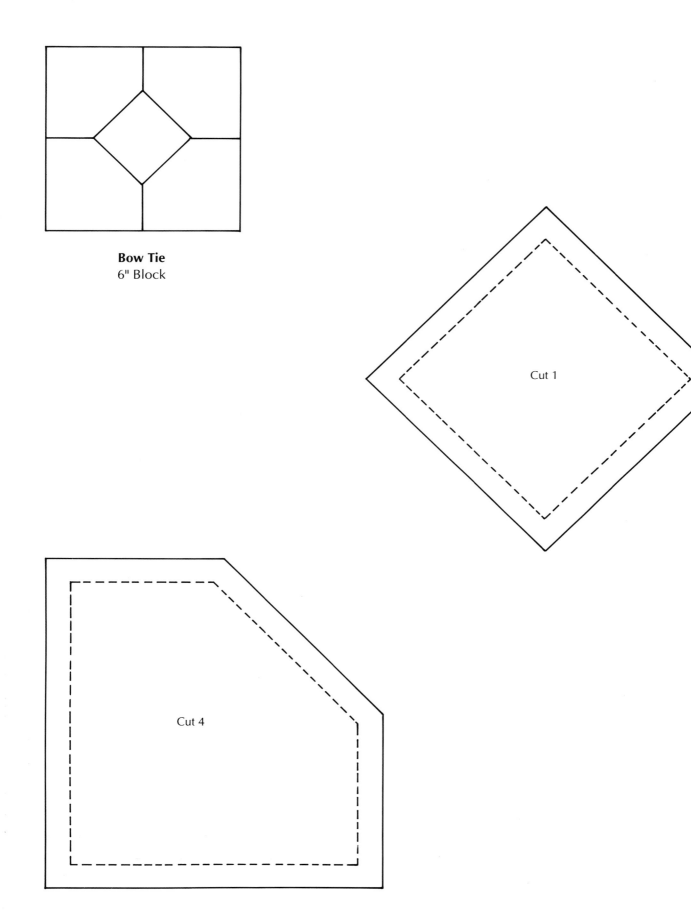

Bow Tie
6" Block

Cut 1

Cut 4

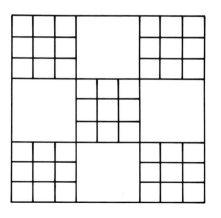

Double Nine-Patch
11 ¼" Block

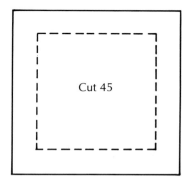

Cut 45

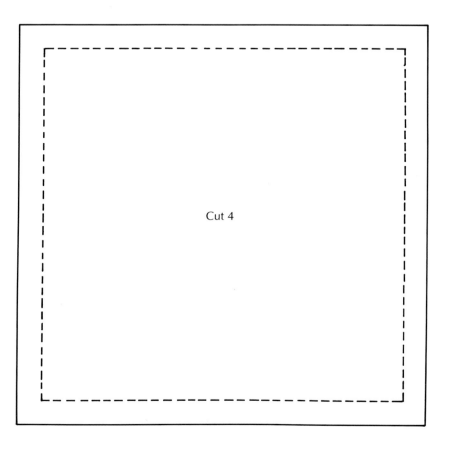

Cut 4

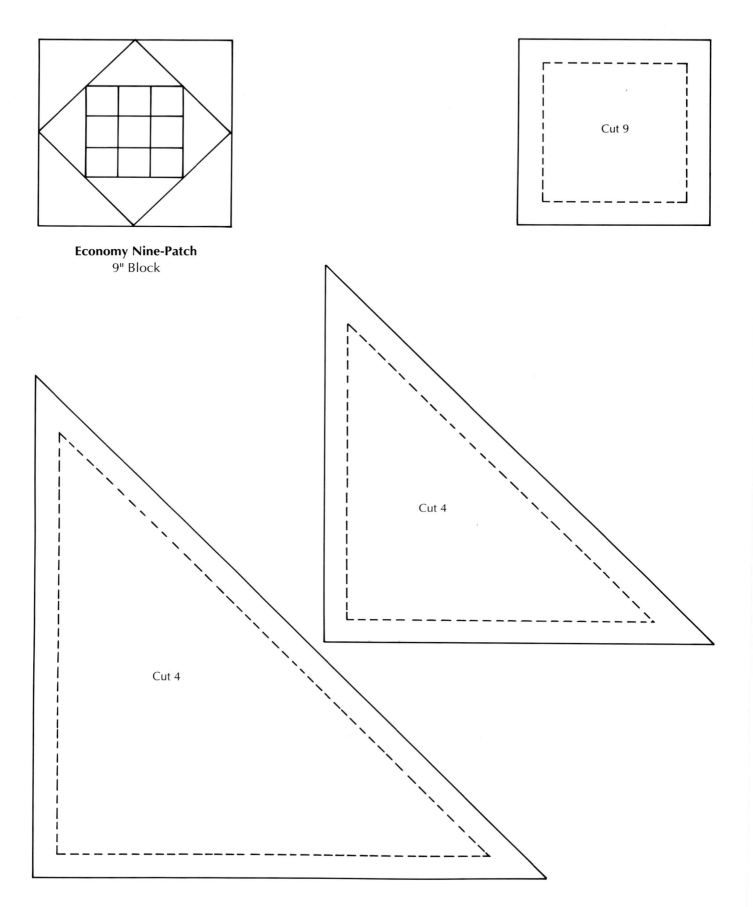

Economy Nine-Patch
9" Block

Cut 9

Cut 4

Cut 4

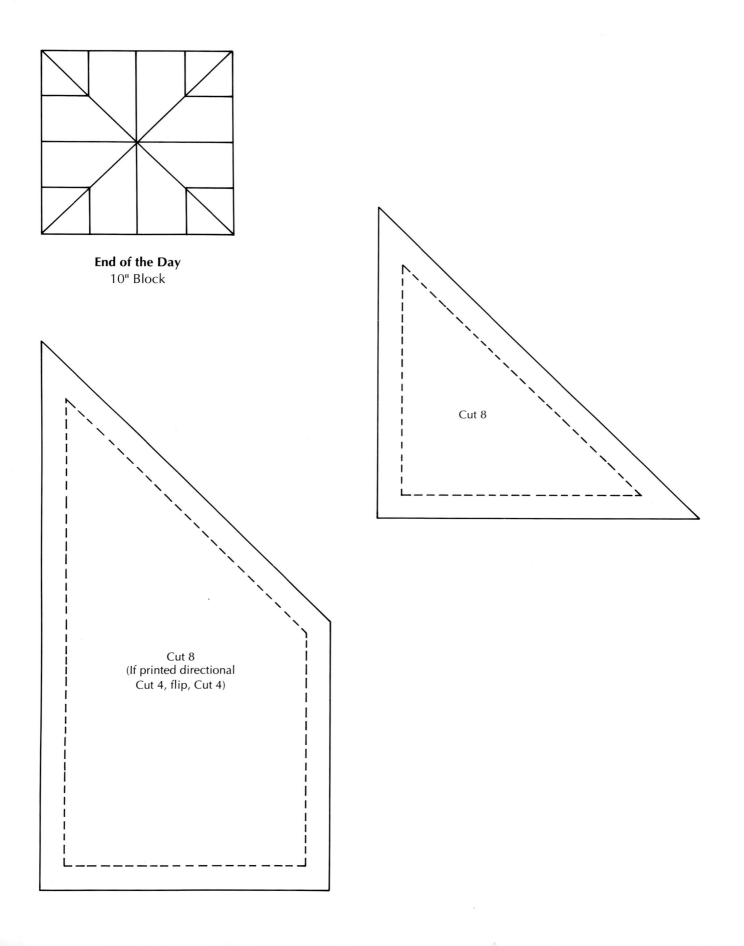

End of the Day
10" Block

Cut 8

Cut 8
(If printed directional
Cut 4, flip, Cut 4)

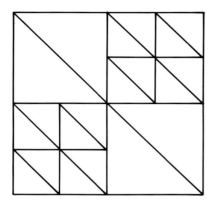

Flock
8" Block

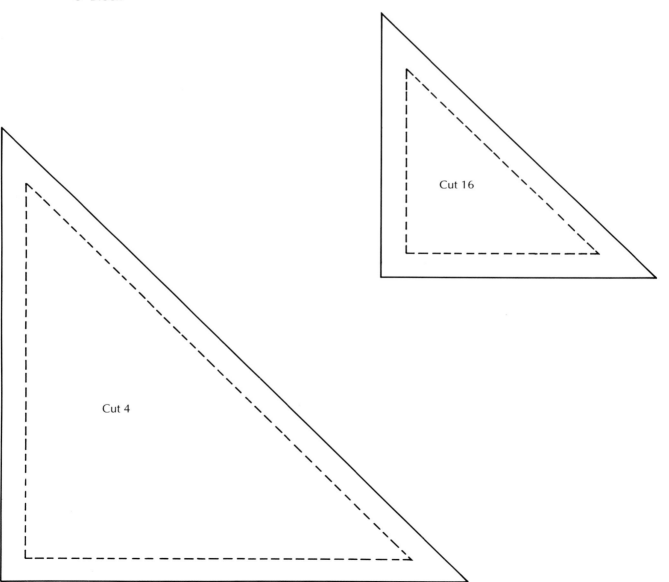

Cut 16

Cut 4

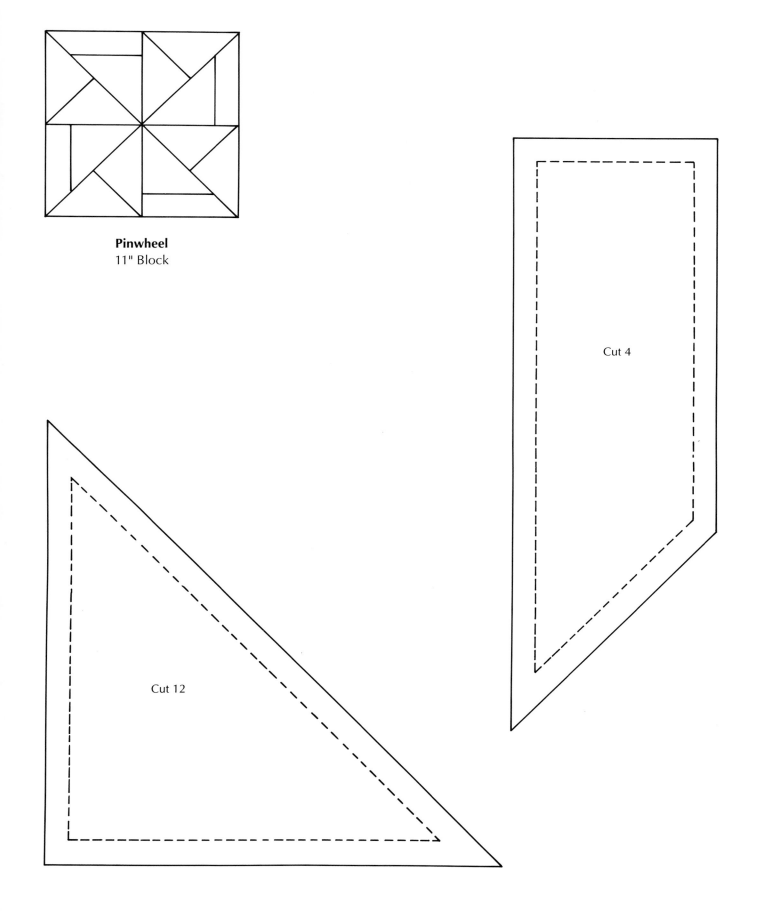

Pinwheel
11" Block

Cut 12

Cut 4

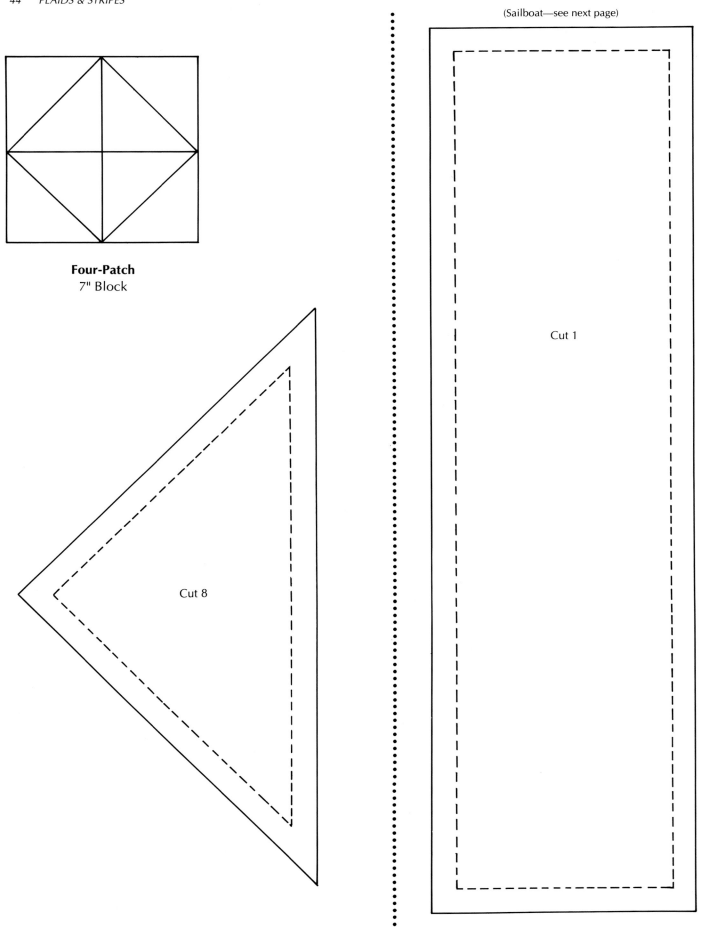

Four-Patch
7" Block

Cut 8

Cut 1

(Sailboat—see next page)

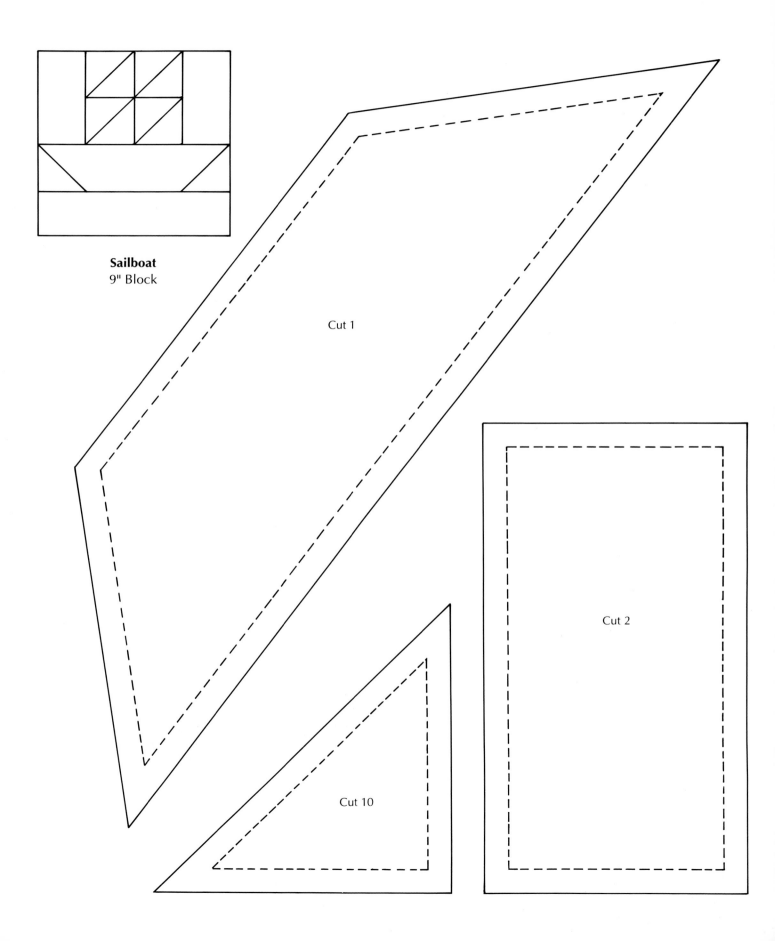

Sailboat
9" Block

Cut 1

Cut 2

Cut 10

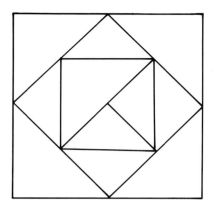

Remembrance Block
8½" Block

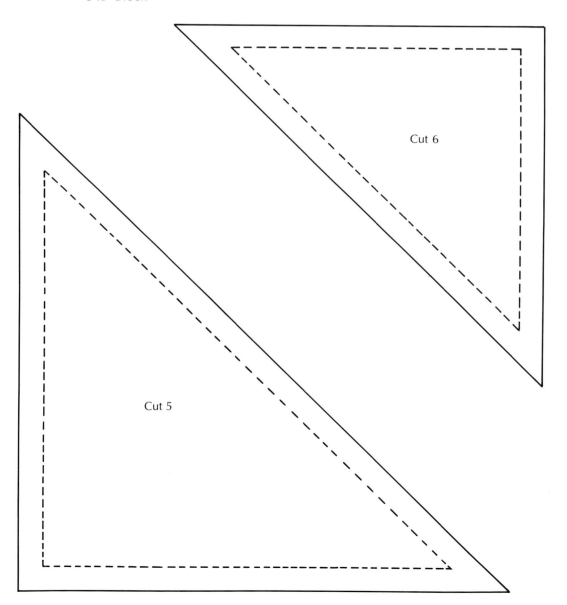

Cut 6

Cut 5

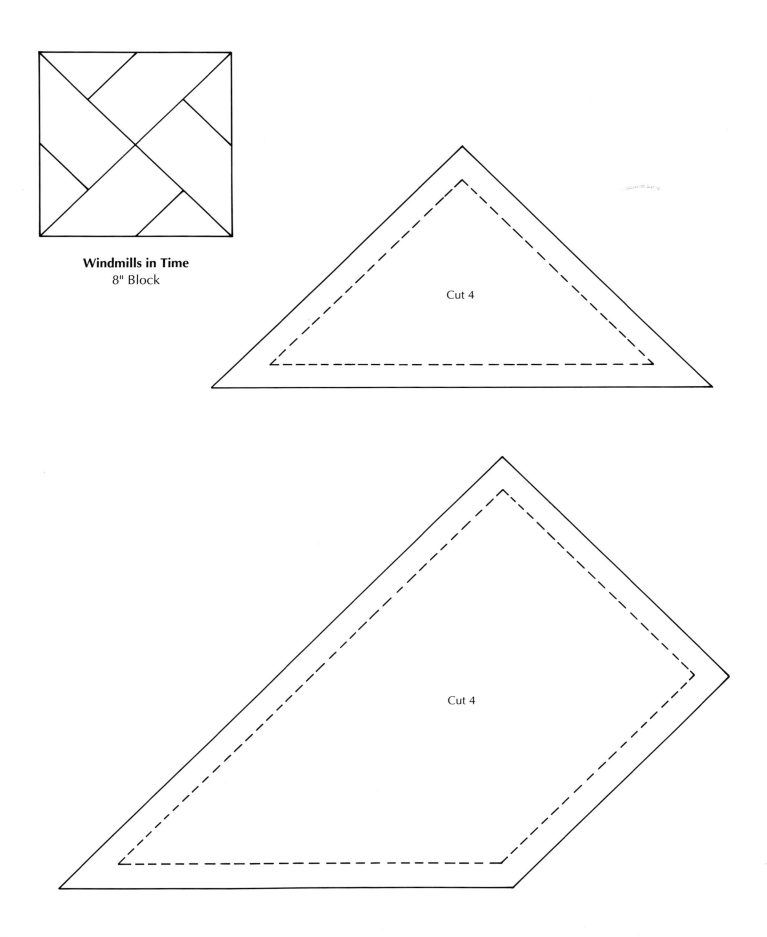

Windmills in Time
8" Block

Cut 4

Cut 4

3

UTILITY QUILTS

The very earliest quilts were probably made strictly to keep someone warm. Somewhere along the line, quilt-makers discovered that quilts could also provide a vehicle for artistic expression. More time and energy were put into the creating process. Fancier, more complicated patterns were chosen. As yard goods became less scarce, better quality fabric was used. Workmanship improved, with more attention being paid to fine and elaborate quilting. Heirloom quilts were born.

But let's back up a minute and pay homage to the quickly made, rougher quilts constructed from the sturdy fabrics at hand. Function, not esthetics, was and is the main concern in the creation of what I call utility quilts, although the somewhat kinder name of country quilts also seems to be coming into use. Addie Barnes' collage-type quilt is an example of the beautiful merging of directionals with solids often found in these quilts (Photo 3.1).

Photo 3.1.   Medallion.
Addie Barnes, Shreveport, LA.
Collection of Eli Leon.

Photo 3.2.   Mississippi String Quilt.
74" x 76". Bertha Brewster, Webster
County, MS, 1930s. Collection of the
author.

During the colonial period, the fabric used would have been stripes, checks, or plaid wool or cotton homespun. Later, corduroy, denim, suiting samples, and even more recently, double knits were added to the stripes and plaids. Those quilts were considered strictly functional and definitely not for display. When used on a bed, they might well have been covered with other, prettier quilts. In the West, cowboys and sheepherders used their quilts as bed rolls. More recently, this type of quilt was often taken on camping and fishing trips.

Historically, these quilts have a variety of names. They are sometimes called comforters, even comfortables. In Pennsylvania and northern England, they were called haps. In Appalachia, the tied variety were called tack quilts, while across the country in New Mexico, quiltmakers used the terms britches quilts, camp quilts, and shoogans.

According to Annette Gero in "The Folklore of the Australian Waggas," utility quilts in that country are commonly called "waggas," perhaps because of the Wagga brand flour sacks from New South Wales that were often used for the stuffing or filling. Other fillings used were old wool socks, or worn coats and suiting, in other words, whatever was past its prime but that could still provide a layer of warmth. The stuffing was covered with either solid or pieced fabric. Wool and cotton plaids and stripes were commonly incorporated.

Utility quilts seem to be associated with pioneer days or periods of lean times. For example, the string quilt in Photo 3.2 was constructed in rural Mississippi during the Great Depression. Utility quilts were created with a sense of frugalness, both of time and of materials. Since these quilts were for warmth and not for beauty, they didn't merit an extended planning period; instead, they were just thrown together, quite often with crude techniques. This feeling of spontaneous creation makes them particularly exciting and appealing to me.

Frequently, these quilts were tied rather than quilted because of the heavy fabrics used. Thick cotton or wool batts, or the rags used for the stuffing, added to the bulk and made such quilts very heavy. See Photo 3.3. In colder areas, wool batt was commonly used. Tacking, rather than quilting, also made it easy to open up the quilt for a periodic cleaning if the batt was wool. And if they *were* hand quilted, the stitch size and length didn't seem as important a consideration as in other, more "serious," types of quilts. In fact, utility quilts were sometimes even machine quilted.

As modern day quiltmakers, we sometimes spend a lot of time planning our projects. We need graph paper, colored pencils, drafting tools, pattern books, plastic template material, access to a photocopy machine...the list goes on and on. Maybe these utility quilts worked because so much wasn't riding on the outcome. A quiltmaker dared to combine together some fabrics that she might normally think twice about using because she didn't have a choice, literally, or she didn't have the time or money to find something better. The quilt needed to be done quickly.

But long before the process of sewing together the quilt itself came the lengthy process of fabric making.

Early homespun quilts were made of woven fabrics, with the choice of design generally limited to stripes, checks, and plaids (Photo 3.4). John Rice Irwin, of Norris, Tennessee, in his *A People and Their Quilts*, outlines the many steps involved.

"Not only did every thread have to be spun on the crude spinning wheel and then woven one by one on the loom. but the steps in preparing and processing the material before spinning were simply prodigious.

"Old timers said that it took at least sixteen months to produce linen fiber. The preparation of the seed bed was initiated in the fall of the year by turning the soil. The flax seed was planted in early spring, and the crop had to be cultivated and weeded throughout the summer until it matured in late summer, or early autumn. It was then pulled and seeded. It was allowed to 'ret' most of the winter, and then it had to be cleaned, re-dried, broken, swingled, and 'hackled' several times in order to remove the woody shell portion from every tiny stalk.

"Cotton had to have every one of the multitudinous seeds removed. Wool had to have the cocklebur and begger lice pulled out by hand, and it had to be washed thoroughly. It has been said that it took ten

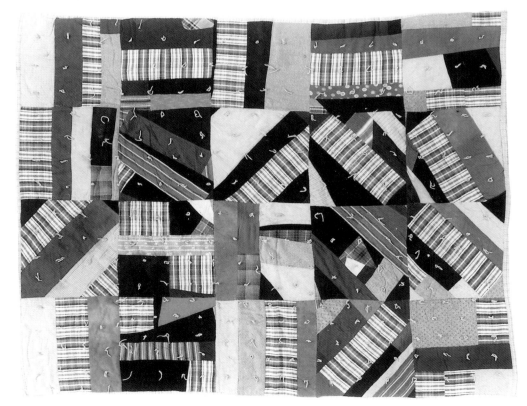

Photo 3.3.   String Quilt.
Collection of Eli Leon.

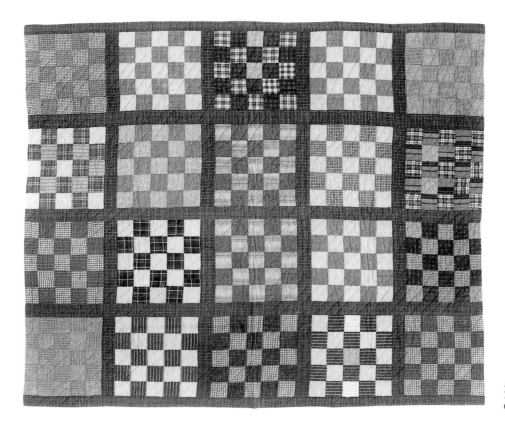

Photo 3.4.   Twenty-five Patch.
74" x 84". New Jersey, 19th Century.
Collection of Peggy Gierke.

times as long to spin thread for a blanket as it did to weave it, and that it took ten times as long to prepare the fiber as it did to spin it. So, several hundred hours were required just to make the cloth for a single quilt."

And we complain about the time it takes to drive to the quilt store to shop for fabric and then to prewash it! It's all relative. It's clear why many early quilts were quite simple. There just wasn't the time to make them more elaborate.

"38 Lines Zigzag" (Color Plate 1A) was inspired by these early homespun quilts. Upon receiving the first shipment of my fabric, I needed to make a sample very quickly. Early quilts I had seen in Nova Scotia provided inspiration for the mood and time period. During that same visit, the Whittier earthquake took place. I had grown up in Whittier, and standing in the classroom hearing about the earthquake, I knew I wanted to make a Streak of Lightning (seismograph) quilt. Hence, the mood, time period, *and* the pattern.

Fortunately, given my time constraints, only a triangle shape was required for the body of the quilt, which was composed in less than two days. My fabric merely needed to be divided into lights and darks. You'll notice the mediums appear on both the light and dark

sides. The border treatment was composed in one-and-a-half days, after the center area was sewn. The backing was created with squares of fabrics leftover from the front, and the pieced binding was built from fabric leftover from the backing. I liked the restrictions inherent in making do. Because of the limitations of time and fabric, there was no agonizing, just doing. However, a bit of modern conveniences helped—I couldn't have worked so quickly without my rotary cutter, my stand-up cutting table, my design wall, and my sewing machine. Nevertheless, by restricting the time and fabric choice, I created my own "pioneer" quilt.

PROJECTS

Try making a quilt with a limited time allotment. We've all felt the pressure of completing a quilt for a contest deadline, for a show, or for presentation as a gift. But I'm talking about a <u>really</u> limited time, such as one or two days, a weekend, perhaps. Make a scenario, if it helps or sounds like fun to you. Imagine you're living in a log cabin on newly cleared land and winter is coming. Or you're in a sod house on the prairie, or in a wagon train going West. My students have especially enjoyed this approach; they seemingly are lifted out of themselves and their ordinary work mode, keeping in mind that their family may well freeze to death if they don't get busy.

Sewing machines and rotary cutters are allowed to speed up the process. And be sure to try freehand cutting. Inaccuracies provide the opportunity to patch and cope or make do.

Working with a single shape, such as the triangle in "38 Lines Zigzag," is the easiest option. Following are some other simple possibilities.

Judy Sogn's "Hit and Miss" (Color Plate 10C) is typical of early quilts that were made in strips. Some African-American quilts also follow this format. The rows are of random width, but everything in one row is identical in width but of varying lengths. Some pieced blocks could also be worked into the composition.

Mata Rolston's "Just Fooling Around" (Color Plate 10A) is a little like the Amish Diamond in a Square format. Early homespun quilts from both Canada and Wales are constructed this way, which is actually just a medallion format. Start in the middle and work out. The blue and tan rectangles at the midpoints of the strips along the diamond edges can be considered coping units, varing in size, when necessary, to accommodate the strips of squares. Mata worked mainly with homespuns to give an older look to her quilt.

Addie Barnes' quilt (Photo 3.1) is an African-American version of the medallion format of working from the center out. In this case, the center shape is rectangular. Follow the seam lines and junctions and you can figure out the order in which the borders were added. Notice that the borders are of unequal width, which adds to the design excitement by creating an unpredictability to the seemingly simple quilt.

Lois Allen's "Hurry, Winter's Coming" (Color Plate 10B), a fine example of a pioneer quilt, provides a good opportunity to combine many different plaids and stripes. The collaged border does a nice job of pulling together the quilt.

Parts of Marion Ongerth's "Still Life with Plaids" (Color Plate 15B) has the feeling of a utility quilt. It was initially begun as the backing for a much more elaborate quilt. At some point, though, the quilt "took off" and became a front. The feeling of spontaneity was exhilarating. And Marion says that half the fun was in making it so quickly after laboring so intensely over the previous quilt.

4

LOG CABIN QUILTS

Log Cabin quilts provide a particularly good place to practice the use of directional fabrics. Because the logs are narrow strips, the impact of any individual fabric is diminished. Many seemingly disparate fabrics can be combined by just adhering to the rules about light and dark placement in your chosen version or rendition. High-contrast-value plaids, and particularly stripes, really show well in the finished quilt.

The "Log Cabin with Courthouse Steps" pictured in Photo 4.1 is one of my all-time favorites. Most of the directionals seem to be on the diagonal. These add nice little touches of activity here and there. Using diagonal cuts of stripes, and also plaids, was a fairly common practice with Log Cabin quilts, probably because they were often contructed by sewing the strips to a backing which added stability.

Betty Kisbey's version of "Lines Pineapple Log Cabin" (Color Plate 11A) has a real antique feeling, perhaps even suggesting that the quilt is made with wool fabric. Identical directional fabrics are repeated in the same order in each block. Betty found that after doing a preliminary mockup, she needed to change the order of the lights. They were originally to be positioned with the lightest in the center going to the darkest on the outside. She found using just the back-ground color of the fabric as a guide didn't work because the lightest background choice actually had darker design lines than the second lightest fabric. When viewed from afar, where visual fusion had a chance to occur, the true lightest fabric read darker than the next choice. The wonderful interior glow that Betty achieved was worth the extra time spent experimenting. Because Betty worked with identical blocks, when she was ready to join units, two matching lights touched each other. Realistically, there's a good chance that these two plaids won't line up perfectly, as they did in Photo 4.2. A nice vibration (the positive description) occurs when the plaids are misaligned, as in Photo 4.3. Notice that there seems to be more vitality in the second pairing.

Log Cabin quilts can be built in many ways. Three exciting African-American versions, where one block is the entire quilt, are seen in Photos 4.4, 4.5, and 4.6. Nancy Washington Wytch's "'X' Medallion" is sometimes called Variation C. The same color is repeated four times as the design spirals around from the center. Another choice is to make the logs only on two sides, as in Louisa Shelbon's "Log Cabin." Or, how about a giant Courthouse Steps, as used by Rachel Adkins. Notice the directional fabrics used in each quilt.

Photo 4.1.   Log Cabin with Courthouse Steps. 30 1/4" x 42 3/4".
Collection of B. J. Welden. Courtesy of Edward Brown.

*Photo 4.2.
Lines Pineapple
Log Cabin* (detail).
60" x 60".
Betty Kisbey,
Sacramento, CA,
1989. Matching
plaids lined up
perfectly at seam.

*Photo 4.3.
Lines Pineapple
Log Cabin* (detail).
60" x 60".
Betty Kisbey,
Sacramento, CA,
1989. Matching
plaids misaligned
at seam create
vibration.

Photo 4.4.   'X' Medallion. Nancy Washington Wytch, Gulfport, MS,
1930s. Collection of Eli Leon.

Photo 4.5. Log Cabin. Louisa Shelbon, Marion, LA. Quilted by Willia Ette Graham, 1985. Collection of Eli Leon.

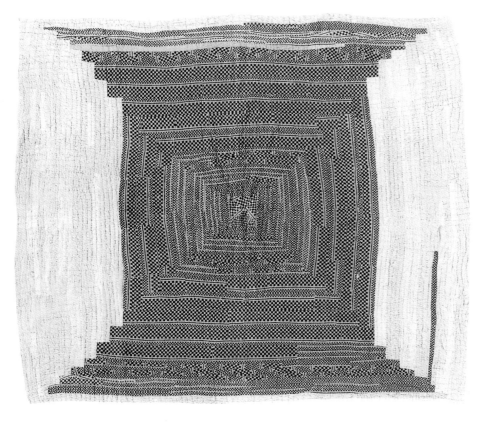

Photo 4.6. Log Cabin. Rachel Adkins, Houston, TX. Collection of Eli Leon.

The Log Cabin approach to assembling also works in more contemporary-feeling quilts. In "Goodbye the Nasturtiums" (Color Plate 16A), I cut the logs freehand. I also started with a shape other than a square for the center (Photo 4.7). The resulting flowers didn't need to be the same size or shape. How the units were ultimately joined with each other was a problem to be dealt with later. The solution was actually fun!

Marion Ongerth made some Log Cabin-like assemblages in "Still Life with Plaids" (Color Plate 15B). The wonderful shapes seem to frolic on the quilt. The blocks were composed right at the sewing machine. Each unit began with a central shape, which didn't happen to be the usual square. Some blocks were sewn in the traditional spiral of a Log Cabin block; some were sewn in a Courthouse Steps fashion of two opposite sides at a time; some were composed in random order. Study Photo 4.8. Frequent interruptions— perhaps annoying at the time—actually added to the end feeling of spontaneity. Marion also didn't adhere to the traditional light and dark placement.

Photo 4.7.   Goodbye the Nasturtiums (detail). 75" x 45". Roberta Horton, Berkeley, CA, 1988. Log Cabin block started with a non-square center and with logs cut freehand.

Photo 4.8.   Still Life with Plaids (detail). 51" x 79". © Marion Ongerth, Berkeley, CA, 1989. Non-traditional Log Cabin-like blocks give a feeling of movement.

AFRICAN-AMERICAN QUILTS

African-American quilts often use directional fabrics freely, even exuberantly. Much study and debate still surrounds this category of quilt as many people struggle to better understand the African-American contribution to the quiltmaking world. Meanwhile, we all can enjoy the spirited nature of these quilts.

Many of the quilts discussed elsewhere in this book were created following European design esthetics, including repetition, symmetry, and balance. Euro-American quilts are constructed of repeat blocks built into grids. If two patterns are used, they are grouped in a checkerboard. Borders, often the same on all edges, heighten the allover feeling of control.

Many African-American quilts look just like those quilts made using the European design esthetics. But African design esthetics also include variation, asymmetry, improvisation, and movement. So, African-American quilts can be composed of more than one block pattern, and variations are common within the block itself. Some of the quilts are assembled in a strip format and, when sashing is used, the impact is often stronger in one direction rather than being of equal importance in both directions. It's a common practice to offset rather than match the intersecting points of the sashing. Sometimes, like units are clustered rather than being evenly divided or balanced throughout the quilt. Borders can be the same on all edges but, as Eli Leon suggests, frequently are not. For example, two opposite borders may match and the other two can be different from the first two and even from each other. In other words, choices and options abound. There's more a feeling of excitement and movement rather than control in African-American quilts.

It's not always easy to identify African-American quilts, unless you know the maker. Look at Photos 3.1, 4.4, 4.5, 4.6, and 6.1. These all are African-American quilts and are made in a variety of styles, including utility, Log Cabin, and appliqué. By carefully studying them, you will notice that they evidence more a feeling of movement as opposed to one of total control. For example, the appliqué quilt by Inena Camp entitled "Boy Bouncing Ball" (Photo 6.1) uses a repeat block format with a regulation lattice sashing. Notice, however, the lack of uniformity in the size of the boy patterns and the variation in their placement within the blocks. Both of these features give a feeling of movement to the quilt.

Essie Sanders' African-American quilt (Photo 5.1) has a wonderful collage feeling. Remnants of four-patches or nine-patches seem to float around within the quilt. Notice her use of directionals within these squares and rectangles. The curved section offered a wonderful coping opportunity. A plaid has been effectively used as a fill-in background to the curved area.

The Arkansas African-American quilt shown in Photo 5.2 is also made with a collage format, although it was actually sewn in three strips. It contains remnants of a Bow Tie block, perhaps recycled from another project. There are also blocks of Rail Fence, Diamond Within a Square, Nine-Patch, and even a few Log Cabins. Matching borders are on opposite edges. Look for the use of directional fabrics, including the light units where the stripes are more subtle.

When repeat blocks are used in an African-American quilt, the result is sometimes quite different than if the same blocks had been assembled in a Euro-American quilt. I find this unique approach to quiltmaking very exciting—it's like a new recipe to me.

Photo 5.1.   Checkerboard. Essie Sanders, Gene Autry, OK.
Collection of Eli Leon.

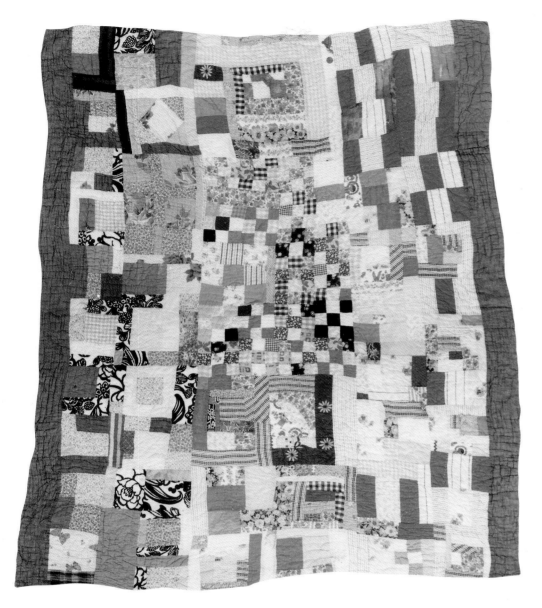

Photo 5.2.   Collage Quilt.
63" x 75". Little Rock, AR,
1950s. Collection of the author.

Their style and energy can be a breath of fresh air for tightly controlled, obsessed quiltmakers.

The African-American quilt made by Versie Harrison (Photo 5.3) is a particularly good example to consider as you design and construct an African-American-inspired quilt. Figure 5.1 is a diagram of the Harrison quilt which has the blocks numbered for easy reference. Not every African-American quilt contains all the ideas/techniques discussed here, although one or more of these ideas/techniques can often be found if you know to look for them.

Gather an assortment of fabrics, remembering to include small, medium, and large prints, solids, and of course, a generous supply of plaids and stripes. Medium- and large-scale prints and off-grain directional fabrics will contribute a feeling of movement. Solids, small-scale prints, and on-grain directional fabrics will bring calm, where necessary. Fabrics don't have to be color co-ordinated. The scrappier, the better.

I have created the following somewhat artificial process to help a quilter unused to working within the freedom of variation, asymmetry, improvisation, and movement to explore the design possibilities of African-American quilts. I find specific directions often help me—or my students—attack a new procedure or put a new thought into use.

Photo 5.3.   Monkey Wrench. Versie Harrison, Oakland, LA.
Collection of Eli Leon.

Block 1: Sew one block of your chosen pattern. Try cutting the shapes freehand, without templates. Look at a drawing of the block drawn to scale for the first block but then discard it. This approach may lead to some distortion (hopefully) when the block is sewn but you may be as amazed as I was to discover how generally accurate the result will be—though your goal here is to *not* be too accurate.

You can use your rotary cutter but hide your ruler or straight edge. Don't bother to true-up any inaccuracies at this point. Think of being on a time limit. Time is too precious a commodity to waste re-doing; always go forward and not backwards.

As additional blocks are made, the fabric may be repeated or new fabric may be introduced. Remember, a certain amount of repetition helps to pull the final quilt together.

1	7	13	19	25	31
2	8	14	20	26	32
3	9	15	21	27	33
4	10	16	22	28	34
5	11	17	23	29	35
6	12	18	24	30	36

Figure 5.1. Versie Harrison *Monkey Wrench* Quilt

Block 2: Make a variation of your chosen pattern. Blocks 1, 16, and 28 in Versie Harrison's quilt are cut from the same shapes but read as separate patterns. See Photo 5.3. Remember, variation is accomplished by changing the value placement within the block.

Block 3: Within this block, make one shape or area larger or smaller; this requires a compensating adjustment in some other area of the block to keep the total finished size the same as the other blocks. Study block 21 in Versie Harrison's quilt (Photo 5.4).

Block 4: When selecting the fabric for this block, make the fabric choice more important than the value choice. In other words, disregard the correct value and put together some fabrics you like, but that are of similar value. The result will be a block in which it's difficult to read the pattern image. Block 26 in Versie Harrison's quilt does this. (See Photo 5.3.) Also notice the nine-patches at the bottom of the quilt. Some units read as a nine-patch while other areas read as a checkerboard.

Block 5: Make the block larger or smaller in total size so that when the quilt is assembled, you will have to add some coping strips. Trimming will be another option, particularly if the removed area can be recycled into another place in the quilt.

Block 6: Introduce a new pattern. By now you are probably becoming bored with your chosen block, anyway, so choose a new pattern. Remember, variation is an esteemed African design esthetic. This block doesn't have to be the same size as the original block. Repeat the process with the first five blocks or wing it. Perhaps you're loosened up enough now to just do it! Your original first block now may look boring to you. Here's some inspiration: Versie Harrison's quilt has an entirely new set of blocks across the bottom!

Make a minimum of nine to twelve total blocks.

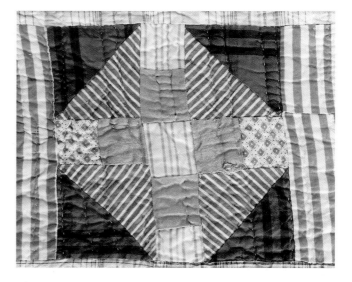

Photo 5.4.   Monkey Wrench (detail). Versie Harrison, Oakland, LA. Collection of Eli Leon.

Now you're ready for the next stage. Because directional fabrics can make a bold statement, they are often useful choices in this process.

Step 1: Arrange the blocks in three vertical rows. Remember to cluster like blocks rather than alternate them.

Step 2: Audition fabric for the two vertical sashes. They may be matching or different. There may be an additional fabric added to get the correct length or to add interest. Don't cut the vertical sashes to their final length until you have completed Steps 3 and 4.

Step 3: Audition fabric for the horizontal sashing. All the fabric may match the vertical sashing, but chances are it will be a new choice or choices. Usually the vertical sashing is the strongest.

Step 4: The vertical rows are the first to be sewn. Start with the row you think will be the longest. It will serve as the "role model" for correct length. All the blocks within that row must now be made the same width. Add necessary coping strips to any blocks that are too narrow. The coping will more likely be added to one edge rather than being evenly divided between two sides. Now join blocks to horizontal sashes, which will be the same width but may vary in height.

Step 5: Sew the other rows. They won't necessarily be the same width as the first row. Each row will be the width of the widest block within that row. Add coping strips if their total length doesn't match the first row sewn. Versie Harrison has used coping strips at the top of the first row and the last two rows.

Step 6: Join the vertical rows to the vertical sashes.

Step 7: Borders may be added with a variety of design choices:
- only on one side
- on two adjacent or opposite sides (matched or mismatched)
- on three sides, all matching, partially matching, or varied
- on four sides, with any combination from above.

Notice the use of plaid fabrics for the vertical sashes in Versie Harrison's quilt. Stripes have been effectively used for many of the horizontal sashes along with four units of a strong diagonal plaid. One border features a plain fabric, another a high-contrast plaid. A strip of nine-patches across the bottom might be considered the third border.

The African-American quilt made by Flossie Kapers (Photo 5.5) is composed of twenty-one blocks, all of which have the same template shapes. See how many variations you can find of the pattern. The horizontal sashes provide the solution as to how twenty-one blocks can be divided into four rows.

"Jordan's Grinning Quilt" by Mary Lou Wright (Color Plate 12B), "Marie Pauline" by George Taylor (Color Plate 12C), and "Rose's Heritage" by Margaret Scott (Color Plate 13A) are all African-American inspired quilts. Each quilter has worked with multiple patterns and a strip format. Mary Lou commented, "I had been apprehensive about trying to make an African-American-inspired quilt because it represented a departure from how I normally work. After completing 'Jordan's Grinning Quilt' I find that I'm not so uptight. I will never be the same."

Dona Cole used the Swahili word for "hello" when naming her quilt "Jumbo" (Color Plate 12A). Notice that the quilt isn't a perfect rectangle, a feature shared with many African-American quilts.

Laura Reinstatler has used a more complicated set for "African-American Study" (Color Plate 13B). The green horizontal sash slashes across the composition, dividing it in an interesting way. The first star block she sewed is located at the bottom of the middle row. Notice how much freer, and exciting, the stars became as she got warmed up to the ideas we have been discussing. Laura, known for her beautifully controlled work in decorative clothing and quilts, commented after completing "African-American Study," "I feel that going through the process of making this quilt facilitated self-exploration in my work. There is much more freedom, spontaneity, and energy in what I do now. The gut level approach I learned with this quilt enables me to make departures more easily."

(See page 81, after Color Section, for Photo 5.5)

A

1

A   *38 Lines Zigzag* (front)
1988. 65" x 81"
Roberta Horton
Berkeley, CA
pieced by Cathie Hoover
and Mary Mashuta
quilted by Janet Bales and
Roberta Horton

B   *38 Lines Zigzag* (back)

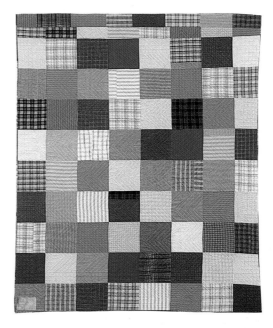

B

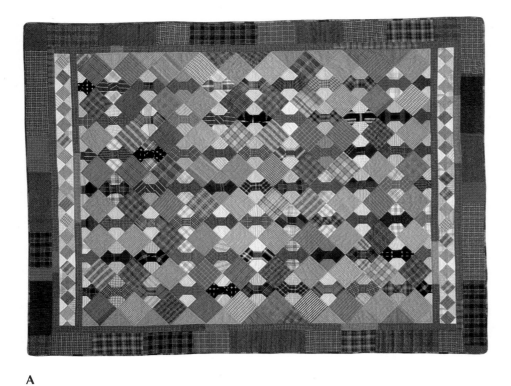

A

2 _____

A *Grandfather's Tie Collection*
1989. 68" x 90"
Elaine Anderson
Castro Valley, CA
quilted by Kristina Volker

B *Tall Pine Trees*
1989. 72" x 102"
Rebecca Weber
Piedmont, CA

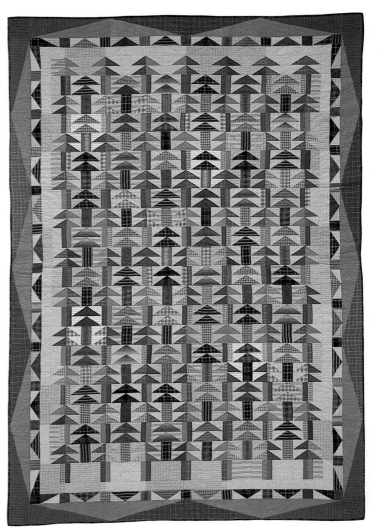

B

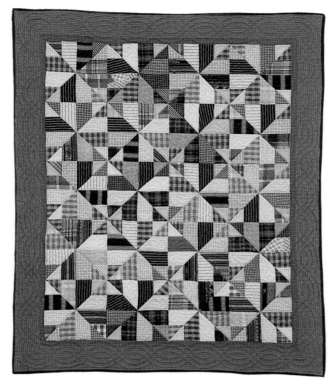

A

B

3

A *End of the Day*
1989. 48" x 57"
Barb Kolby
Bellingham, WA

B *Plaids and Lines*
1988. 29" x 35 ½"
Charisa Martin Anderson
Lynnwood, WA

C *Windmills in Time*
1989. 40" x 48 ½"
Kathy Ezell
Lynnwood, WA

C

A

4

A   *Remembrance in Plaids*
1989. 64" x 79 ½"
Charlene Phenney
McMillan, WA

B   *Antique Double Nine-Patch*
1989. 85" x 103"
Quilt Lovers Group
of Marin Needle
Arts Guild
San Rafael, CA

B

A

B

5

A *Flock of Geese*
1989. 57" x 73 ½"
Nancy Mahoney
Seattle, WA

B *Journey's End*
1989. 27 ½" x 40"
Betty Mensinger
Surrey, British Columbia,
Canada

C *Roberta's Neighborhood*
1989. 54" x 65"
Barbara Dallas
Moraga, CA

C

A

6

A *Angles and Squares*
1989. 30" x 38"
Marilyn Reardon
Seattle, WA

B *Angles and Squares*
1989. 49" x 61"
Suzanne Lucy
Deming, WA

B

7

A *Stars in Stripes*
1989. 36" x 48"
Joyce Miller
Edmonds, WA

B *Pinwheel*
1989. 67" x 57"
Mata Rolston
Davis, CA

C *Hearts '86*
1986. 22" x 26"
Annette Anderson
Deming, WA

A

B

C

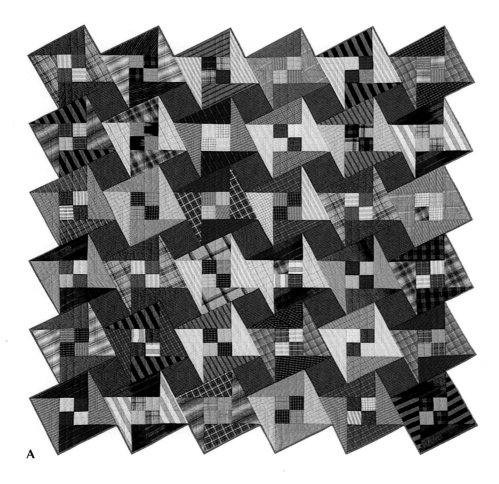

A

8

A *Plaid Lattice*
1989. 61" x 61"
Rebecca Rohrkaste
Berkeley, CA

B *Fabric Sails*
1989. 63" x 40"
Paula Fluder
Puyallup, WA

B

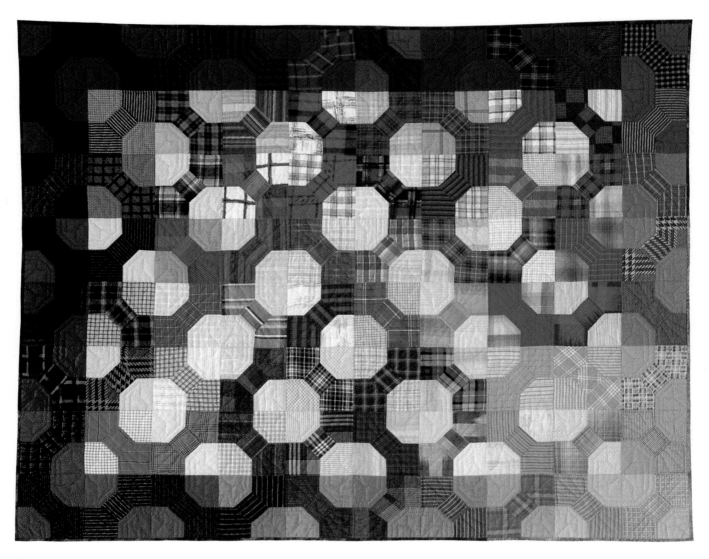

A

9

A *Plaids on Hand* (front)
1989. 59" x 47"
Roberta Horton
Berkeley, CA
pieced by Mary Mashuta
quilted by Janet Bales

B *Plaids on Hand* (back)

B

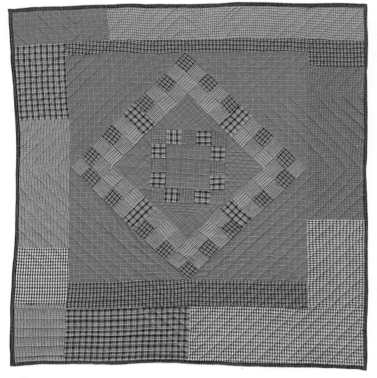

A

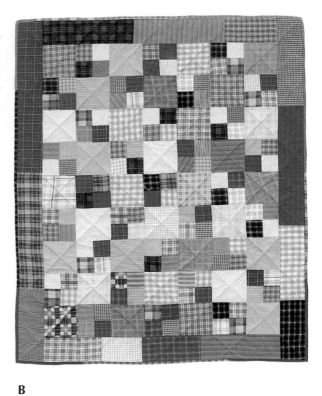

B

C

10

A *Just Fooling Around*
1989. 44" x 47"
Mata Rolston
Davis, CA

B *Hurry, Winter's Coming*
1989. 34" x 41 ½"
Lois Allen
Davis, CA

C *Hit and Miss*
1989. 39" x 50"
Judy Sogn
Seattle, WA

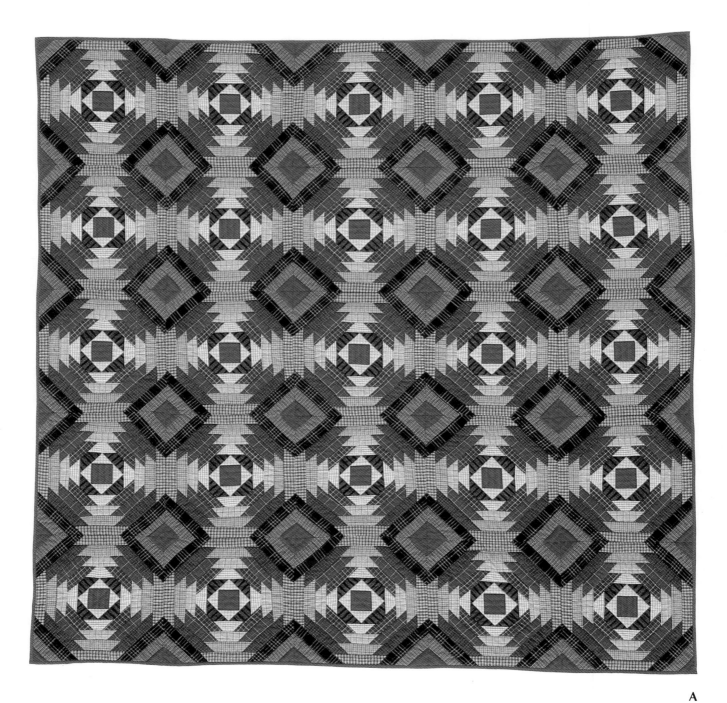

A

11

A *Lines Pineapple Log Cabin*
1989. 60" x 60"
Betty Kisbey
Sacramento, CA
quilted by Kristina Volker

A

B

12

A *Jumbo ('Hello')*
1989. 34" x 69"
Dona Graf Cole
Marietta, GA

B *Jordan's Grinning Quilt*
1987. 56" x 51"
Mary Lou Wright
Marysville, WA

C *Marie Pauline*
1989. 38" x 65"
George Taylor
Anchorage, AK

C

A

B

13
_____

A *Rose's Heritage*
1988. 41" x 45"
Margaret Gilmore Scott
Danville, CA

B *African-American Study*
1989. 41" x 45"
Laura Munson Reinstatler
Mill Creek, WA

A

14

A   *Princeton Nine-Patch*
1989. 69" x 104"
Joan Sextro
Albany, CA

B   *Square Within a Square*
1988. 49½" x 52"
Elaine Anderson
Castro Valley, CA

B

15

A *Walk on the Wild Side*
1988. 59" x 51"
© Marion Ongerth
Berkeley, CA

B *Still Life with Plaids*
1989. 51" x 79"
© Marion Ongerth
Berkeley, CA

A

B

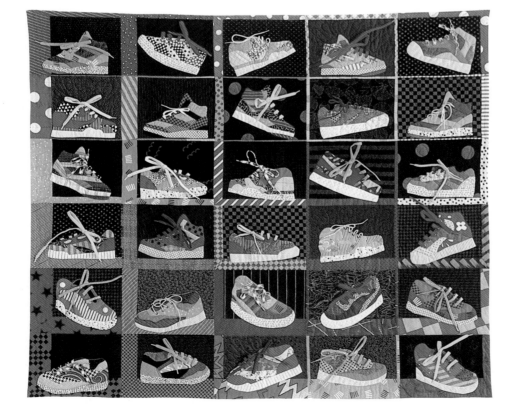

A

16

A *Goodbye the Nasturtiums*
1988. 75" x 45"
Roberta Horton
Berkeley, CA
quilted by Roberta Horton
and Janet Bales

B *Plaid Forest*
1989. 45" x 32 1/2"
©Ruth B. McDowell
Winchester, MA
(Photo by David Caras)

B

Photo 5.5. Double Strip. Flossie H. Kapers, Haynesville, LA, 1980s.
Collection of Eli Leon.

6

APPLIQUÉ

A fellow quilter once complimented me on my first collection of plaids and stripes, adding how much she would like to use them, but, alas, she was embarking on an appliqué quilt. "Of course you don't use plaids in appliqué," she said.

I just was not ready to accept such sweeping certitude. So, as I looked through quilt books and calendars, I found myself searching for older appliqué quilts that featured directional fabrics. Sure enough, they exist! There wasn't—and isn't—an unwritten rule against the use of plaids and stripes in appliqué. "Don't use directionals in beginning quilts...don't use plaids

and stripes in appliqué...." Where *do* these mistaken notions come from? In the great "What if" tradition, push these timeworn concepts to their limits, and if they don't work for you, push them away.

Look at Inena Camp's charming quilt, "Boy Bouncing Ball" (Photo 6.1). The stripe figure feels more controlled while the plaid figure shows more movement. Both blocks present an interesting contrast to the solids and prints used in the rest of the quilt. Her quilt is a good indication that everything I've said about plaids and stripes in pieced quilts can apply to their use in appliqué. Let's look at some other innovative directions taken by today's quilting appliquérs.

Pat Cox has created traditional looking flowers with plaids and stripes in "Plaid Floral Wreath." Interest is

Photo 6.1.   *Boy Bouncing Ball.* Inena Camp, Chesnee, SC, 1930s. Collection of Eli Leon.

Photo 6.2.   *Plaid Floral Wreath* (unquilted top, detail). 44" x 60". Pat Cox, Minneapolis, MN, 1989.

Photo 6.3. *It's Not Necessarily Xmas* (unquilted top, detail). 52" x 52". Pat Cox, Minneapolis, MN, 1989.

achieved within the bouquet by varying the scale and the patterns of the weave (Photo 6.2). In the red and green quilt "It's Not Necessarily Xmas," Pat has appliquéd printed roses into a crazy quilt basket for a new, but still traditional look (Photo 6.3).

Nancy Freeman specializes in making machine appliqué pictures using many wonderful fabrics. Look at "Bette's Oceanview Diner" (Photo 6.4). Notice how cleverly the plaid fabric is used in the skirt of the seated woman. By using three pieces cut at different angles, she is able to accentuate the fullness of the skirt.

Marion Ongerth used plenty of directionals in "Walk on the Wild Side" (Color Plate 15A). The "Roberta Horton Block" features scraps from the first batch of my Lines Collection (Photo 6.5). The contrast of scale and pattern of the four plaids and the two stripes is particularly pleasing. And, of course, the plaid shoelace is just right. Marion has managed to combine many other fabrics in the quilt. Notice how the directionals tone down some of the wild, wonderful choices.

Photo 6.4. *Bette's Oceanview Diner.* 24" x 18". Nancy Freeman, Alamo, CA, 1983. (Photo by Nancy Freeman.)

Photo 6.5.   *Walk on the Wild Side* (detail). 59" x 51".
© Marion Ongerth, Berkeley, CA, 1988.

In "Still Life with Plaids" (Color Plate 15B), Marion Ongerth has restricted herself just to directional fabrics for her composition. She commented, "These plaids are a lot of fun to work with. They're addictive; you can't stop! I'm really hooked." Notice how simple the design of the appliqué area of the quilt is. A shape like a leaf is perfect to practice combining directionals. Marion has used her machine for both the satin stitch of the appliqué and for an embellishing stitch. Study Photo 6.6.

Photo 6.6.   *Still Life with Plaids* (detail). 51" x 79".
© Marion Ongerth, Berkeley, CA, 1989.

APPLIQUÉ PATTERNS

Appliqué patterns are easy to make because all you need is the outline or silhouette of the proposed shape. Newspapers, magazines, catalogs, and books abound with subjects. Watch for flat line drawings (like those used in advertising); these are far easier to copy than photographs which show dimension. Marvelous pattern source books are also available, such as those from Dover Publishing. (Their Pictorial Archive Series allows reproduction of up to ten plates or parts on any one product without written permission. Generally, projects for personal use and not for sale don't require permission.)

What stops most quilters from using these widely available sources is the difficulty of the design not being the correct size for their project. Some quilters fiddle with photocopy machines, though you can run up quite a bill getting the size exactly right. Just as there was a method for enlarging pieced patterns, there is also one for appliqué.

Enlargement Method:

1. Trace the proposed shape onto plain paper. Measure the widest part of the design. Using this measurement, form a square around the design. The square should touch the design on two sides. Cut out this square.

2. Make a second square the desired size of your design. (This won't be the size of the block but will be how much space the design will fill up in the block.) Cut out this second square (Figure 6.1).

Draw Square Around Shape   Draw Square Desired Size

Figure 6.1.

3. Go through the following procedure with both paper squares: fold each one in half, then repeat folding three more times so you end up with sixteen equal divisions when each paper is opened. Draw with a ruler along the creases to form a grid on both squares.

4. Pay attention to the same division on both papers at one time. Put dots on the second paper where the drawing intersects the lines on the first paper. Starting in the upper left-hand corner of the second paper, move around the paper until all the necessary dots have been marked (Figure 6.2).

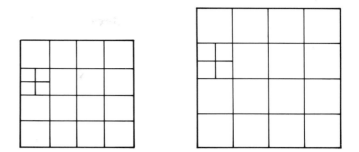

Figure 6.3.   Subdivide in Complicated Areas

will find this step vastly improves the result, since it tends to correct or smooth out lines. You now have an appliqué pattern. Don't forget to add the seam allowance if you're doing hand appliqué.

Paper-Cut Method:

One of my favorite methods of obtaining a design is through paper cutting. Armed with some good paper-cutting scissors and some plain newsprint, I cut away until I obtain a usable shape. Think of yourself as a sculptor starting to chisel on a new block of marble. Somewhere inside is the statue; you as the sculptor only need to chip away the excess. I use two basic methods for paper cutting: one for symmetrical shapes and one for asymmetrical shapes.

Symmetrical Shapes

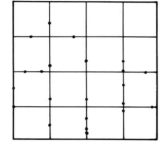

Figure 6.2.   Place Dots Where Drawing Intersects Lines

5. Always work in pencil and keep an eraser handy. Connect the dots to form the shape. If there is too much activity in one division, you may have to subdivide that square into a four-patch on both pieces of paper. This will give you a few more places for the design to intersect. You should now have an approximation of your desired shape (Figure 6.3).

6. Fine tune your design. Check for accuracy with the original. Sometimes the changes you accidentally made will actually look better. Use the broad side of your pencil or a fat felt-tip marker to go around the outline. You

1. Start with the paper the size needed for the design, whether it be a square or rectangle. Since many designs are symmetrical, fold the paper in half before cutting. Then you only need to come up with half of the shape; the second half is automatic.

2. Look at a design source for inspiration and guidance. Or, try cutting from your imagination. Shapes such as a heart, tulip, or butterfly are shapes you probably can cut from memory. (Don't tune out. Try it first, you may surprise yourself how easy this is to do!) When you cut, remember the edge of the paper is a guideline for your desired size. Try to cut near the edges rather than close to the fold.

3. Open the paper and look at the shape. You should have an immediate reaction: it's too fat, or too skinny, etc. Cut a second shape, taking the fine advice you just gave yourself. It may take several attempts before you're satisfied, but at least no erasing is involved!

4. If you'll be doing hand appliqué, remember to add the seam allowance while cutting the shape from fabric.

Asymmetrical Shapes

1. Proceed as above except don't fold the paper in half. You will probably need to look at a design source.

2. Remember to make your paper the size of the desired shape and to add the seam allowance before cutting the fabric if you'll be doing hand appliqué.

BEGINNING APPLIQUÉ PROJECT

Annette Anderson's "Hearts '86" (Color Plate 7C) is a perfect beginning project for using directional fabrics

in appliqué because both the background and the appliqué shapes use plaids and stripes. Here's the procedure:

1. Cut twenty background squares (4½") to form a checkerboard of light and dark units, most cut on-grain. Arrange them in a pleasing fashion on your design wall.

2. Cut twenty hearts from various directional fabrics. Use either a pattern cut from a 3" square or cut freehand from a 3" piece of fabric. The second approach lends even more of a folk art feeling to the finished piece.

3. Arrange and rearrange the hearts on the background squares until you come up with some interesting combinations. See Photo 6.7.

4. For hassle-free appliqué, try the following:
   a. Using an X shape, baste a heart to a square. Don't bother to baste all around the edge. See Figure 6.4.

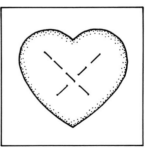

Figure 6.4.   Basting

Photo 6.7.   Hearts '86 (detail). 22" x 26". Annette Anderson, Deming, WA, 1986.

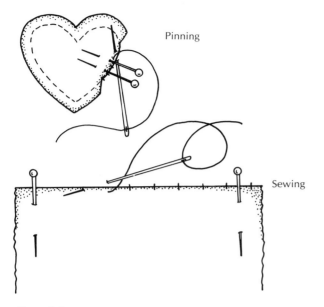

Pinning

Sewing

Figure 6.5.

b. Turn under the seam allowance and hold it in place with pins placed perpendicular to the edge. Only work on a 2" or 3" section at a time. Use a hidden hemming stitch, with thread matching the appliqué shape. Stitches should be about ⅛" apart (Figure 6.5).

c. Convex curved areas (those that protrude out) will need some fullness eased in because you're turning a larger area into a smaller area. Turn under the seam allowance; feel for lumps. Place the piece flat on your worktable. Position your fingers on both sides of the lumpy area. Run the blunt end of a needle under the seam allowance, pulling gently up toward you. The tension created will allow you to redistribute the fullness. Pin. (Never clip this type of curve!) See Figure 6.6.

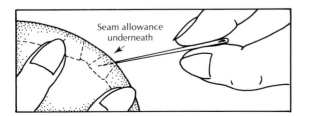

Seam allowance underneath

Figure 6.6. Convex Curves

d. Concave curves (those that go into the shape) may require clipping to release the tension as you turn under the seam allowance from a smaller area into a larger area. Cuts should be less than the ¼" seam allowance. Make a minimum of cuts; it's better to have to add more if the curve is still too tight. Make stitches closer together in this area (Figure 6.7).

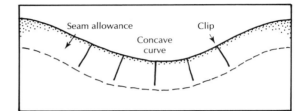

Seam allowance   Clip

Concave curve

Figure 6.7. Concave Curves

e. Turning corners is done in three stages. Fold under the seam allowance to the end of side #1, and trim any fabric that extends beyond side #2. Next, fold under a triangle at the tip; stitch to the point. Finally, fold under side #2. Put more stitches in this area to firmly anchor it (Figure 6.8).

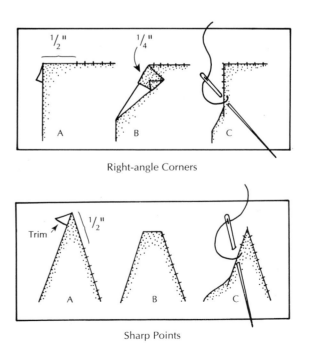

½"   ¼"

A   B   C

Right-angle Corners

Trim   ½"

A   B   C

Sharp Points

Figure 6.8. Turning Corners

7

CONTEMPORARY QUILTS

Any quilt made today could rightly be called a contemporary quilt. Remember, our quilts are a reflection of who we are, where we live, and the time period in which we live. My definition of a contemporary quilt (at least those that I'll discuss in this chapter) is that it must be constructed of woven fabric and the subject matter must be original in content, that is, come from the mind of the quiltmaker.

Ruth McDowell's "Plaid Forest" (Color Plate 16B) is a beautiful contemporary quilt just filled with direc-

tional fabrics. As she was designing it, she found it difficult to achieve the feeling of dancing lights seen in a forest. Most printed fabrics read as too solid when viewed from afar. Ruth liked the way plaids looked in her friend Rhoda Cohen's quilts; when she decided to try some herself, Rhoda suggested she place the plaids off-grain. Ruth said this simple suggestion proved a real breakthrough. Suddenly, there was the light effect she was trying to capture.

Ruth's "Plaid Forest" is nicely bordered with a

Photo 7.1. Square Within a Square. 49½" x 52". Elaine Anderson, Castro Valley, CA, 1988. Outline of the original composition of the quilt.

muted, calm print. A small amount of appliqué in the bottom area of the border adds dimension. The viewer gets the feeling of walking in to the quilt.

Sometimes a quilt feels contemporary because the borders aren't handled in a traditional, balanced approach. Elaine Anderson's "Square Within a Square" is a good example (Color Plate 14B). The border represents a hefty percentage of the quilt. Photo 7.1 shows an outline of the original composition of the quilt. Elaine was able to achieve a wonderful spatial illusion of a twisting diamond by adding triangles onto the four edges of the quilt body; that allows the eye to then pick out that shape in the interior. Her plaid is used in a very minimalist way. Fortunately her choice was a bold, high contrast, large-scale plaid that shows well.

"Black and White Series #7" (Photo 7.2) by Leslie Carabas suggests the drama possible with bold, high contrast stripes. The buoyancy of the polka dots plays well against the rigidness of the stripes. Notice the offsetting of the stripes when the same fabric is repeated nearby.

Photo 7.2.   Black and White Series #7. 10½" x 12½".
© Leslie C. Carabas, Berkeley, CA, 1988.

"Goodbye the Nasturtiums" (Color Plate 16A) is a quilt I felt compelled to make after visiting one of my favorite coastal towns, Mendocino, in northern California. As a city girl, I enjoy its funky rundown qualities. On this particular trip, the town was more beautiful than ever, with designer flowers everywhere. So this quilt was to become a statement about the "yuppification" of bucolic Mendocino.

Photo 7.3.   Goodbye the Nasturtiums (detail). 75" x 45".
Roberta Horton, Berkeley, CA, 1988.

I was particularly interested in combining some of my oldest, most traditional prints (to represent "old" Mendocino) with some more modern and contemporary prints (to suggest the "yuppie" influence). I also liked to think of the process as a revitalizing of my tired, older fabric. Plaids and stripes were used generously to act as a bridge between the fabrics (Photo 7.3). The abstract composition is held together with a large-scale plaid border.

Marion Ongerth's complex appliqué composition "Monday" (Photo 7.4) uses a liberal amount of directionals. It was the first time Marion made a real effort to use plaids on a large scale. She had willingly bought stripes for years, but for some reason hadn't seen the design potential for plaids. Marion said, "I'm surprised how easy plaids are to work with. I didn't know I could put so many together." Some of these fabrics, seen strictly as yardage, are very unappealing. In other words, you must cut into the plaids and stripes to find their magic. Step back and see what they are doing in the composition.

Photo 7.4.   Monday (unquilted top). 58" x 78".
© Marion Ongerth, Berkeley, CA, 1989.

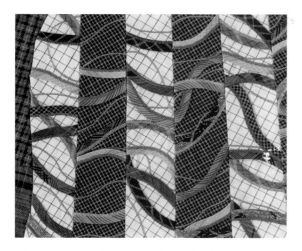

Photo 7.5. *Monday* (unquilted top, detail). 58" x 78".
© Marion Ongerth, Berkeley, CA, 1989.

Study the detail of the skirt in the quilt shown in Photo 7.5. Notice what an effective foil the light and dark small-scale plaid panels provide for the movement of the bias strips. Grainline was kept consistent within the three areas of light plaid and within the three areas

of dark plaid, although the lights and darks aren't aligned. The fabric strips, themselves composed of mostly bias directionals, undulate across the area in an exciting way. What a wonderful feast of plaids and stripes!

In "Quake of '89" by Mary Mashuta (Photo 7.6), plaids and stripes have been used to represent buildings. By placing some of the directionals on-grain while others are used off-grain, she has suggested the requisite feeling of building displacement. The curvilinear prints and the hand-dyed fabrics, used to suggest fire, successfully re-create the havoc of the Marina fire in San Francisco. Mary had formerly used stripes in a far more structured and controlled way to create optical illusions in pieced clothing. In this quilt, she was eager to use stripes and plaids in a more spontaneous way. Notice that most of the directionals she selected are ikats.

One of the seeming hallmarks of the makers of contemporary quilts is their desire to use fabrics beyond the traditional calicos and solids. Let's explore some of the possibilities and see how plaids and stripes can be used to complement these fabrics.

Photo 7.6. *Quake of '89* (detail). 43 1/2" x 57 1/2". Mary Mashuta, Berkeley, CA, 1989.

Large-scale florals are frequently seen today, ranging from classical chintzes to more abstract bouquets. These big designs give a feeling of tremendous movement because of the presence of curved lines; several florals used next to each other causes them to blend into one area of design, making it difficult to differentiate one unique pattern from another (Photo 7.7). The stark simplicity of the simplest plaids and stripes can add a welcome contrast. See Photo 7.8.

Photo 7.7.
Large-scale
Florals

Photo 7.9.
Tropical and
Jungle Scenes

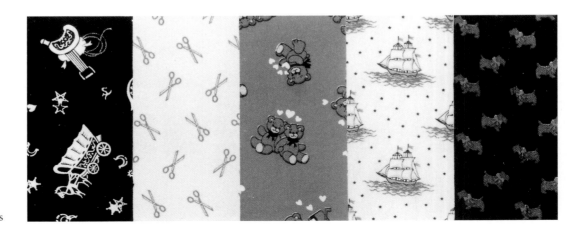

Photo 7.11.
Novelty Prints

Large-scale tropical and jungle scenes are also popular. Although the individual motifs themselves mightn't be big, the overall feeling is one of largeness in contrast to sedate little calico prints. Again, a feeling of movement and confusion results when they are used in close proximity (Photo 7.9). Calming directionals should be selected, probably small-scale or starkly bold (Photo 7.10).

Another contemporary category of fabric is novelty prints. The subject matter varies tremendously. These

Photo 7.8.
Large-scale Florals +
Directionals

Photo 7.10.
Tropical and Jungle
Scenes + Directionals

Photo 7.12.
Novelty Prints +
Directionals

Photo 7.13.
Hand-dyed Fabrics

Photo 7.14.
Hand-dyed Fabrics +
Directionals

Photo 7.15A.
Possible fabric scenarios combining large-scale
florals, tropical or jungle scenes, novelty prints,
calicos, and hand-dyed fabrics with some plaids
and stripes. (See Photos 7.15B and C on facing page.)

are a lot of fun to look at because of their uniqueness but too many spoil the impact (Photo 7.11). Dilute them with a good helping of plaids and stripes. Here, you should be able to use some of the busier directionals because novelty prints aren't always large-scale, and hence busy (Photo 7.12).

The use of hand-dyed fabrics is becoming very popular in quiltmaking. Here I refer not to those that are a solid color, but rather those that have some kind of pattern. In contrast to commercially produced fabric, the patterning of hand-dyed fabrics seems to be more fluid and irregular (Photo 7.13). Too many, though, can cancel their effectiveness. The solidity and stability of directionals used on-grain can allow the viewer to better appreciate the beauty of the ethereal hand-dyed fabrics (Photo 7.14).

Ultimately, our challenge might be to use all these categories of fabric, plus calicos and solids, together within a quilt. Don't forget the necessity of adding some mercurial plaids and stripes to the composition (Photo 7.15A-C). They can calm or intensify, mute or highlight, any fabric pattern.

Photo 7.15B.

Photo 7.15C.

SETS AND BORDERS

A lot can happen between the stage of finishing the blocks for a quilt and actually getting out to the edge of that quilt. Some quilts merely have the blocks joined together, as in Barb Kolby's "End of the Day" (Color Plate 3A), a technique that allows the viewer to seek, and to find, all sorts of pattern variations. Because she composed her quilt in a very scrappy way, one is drawn in, wondering "What *is* the pattern?" The blocks were interesting enough without any embellishment. The border isn't eye-catching, and it doesn't need to be. In fact, it would detract from the body of the quilt if it were. The solutions to questions of setting (how to join blocks) and borders (how to frame a quilt) aren't always so simple.

SETS

How we choose to position the blocks within a quilt is referred to as setting the quilt. Options include placing the blocks parallel or perpendicular to the edge, sewing them directly to each other, or adding new design elements such as sashing, alternate plain blocks, or alternate pieced blocks. Let's explore some of the possibilities.

Photo 8.1.   Tall Pine Trees (detail). 72" x 102". Rebecca Weber, Piedmont, CA, 1989. The line defines the edges of one block.

Photo 8.2.   The Trees. 33" x 31". Connie Nordstrom, Farmington, NM, 1989.

Kathy Ezell's "Windmills in Time" (Color Plate 3C) features mirror image blocks that form a visual interwoven lattice when the blocks are joined side-by-side. Nothing fancy could be added to the blocks without destroying their impact. Again, a simple solution is best because of the chosen pattern.

Sometimes a greater allover image is created when the blocks are routinely joined. It's only when the blocks are attached that the visual magic happens. In other words, it's free! Look at Rebecca Weber's "Tall Pine Trees" (Color Plate 2B). By carefully studying the actual pattern (Photo 8.1), we see that the perimeter rectangles and triangles are starting to form other trees. This is represented by color changes in the actual quilt although one is not initially aware that some trunks and trees are composed of one color while others are split to show two colors.

Connie Nordstrom also worked with a tree block (Photo 8.2). The bottom of her block actually suggests both the ground for the trees and a visual horizontal lattice. See Figure 8.1.

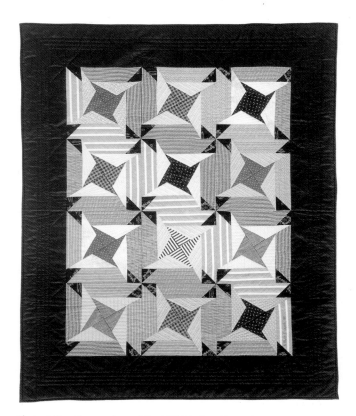

Photo 8.3.   Razzmatazz. 41" x 50". Marion Ongerth, Berkeley, CA, 1985.

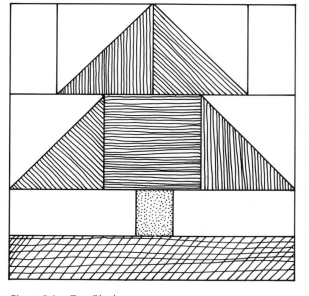

Figure 8.1.   Tree Block

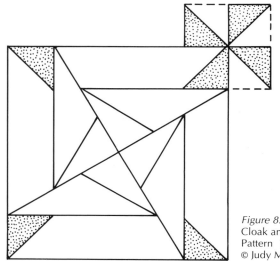

Figure 8.2.
Cloak and Dagger
Pattern 1983
© Judy Martin

Sometimes a block has a built-in lattice that isn't apparent when looking at the individual block. Another example of such a "freebie" is the Cloak and Dagger block used by Marion Ongerth in "Razzmatazz" (Photo 8.3). A multicolored lattice with a pinwheel intersection is formed from the joined blocks (Figure 8.2).

Betty Mensinger chose a block which turns into an automatic diagonal lattice in "Journey's End." Visually, one sees intimations of a Flying Geese pattern. See Color Plate 5B.

In the quilts discussed so far, the blocks have been merely joined together in a straightforward way. The

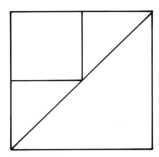

Figure 8.3.
Angles and Squares Block

selected patterns have created the magic. Some patterns can change drastically if we have them set parallel to the edge or on point. Both Marilyn Reardon and Suzanne Lucy used an Angles and Squares block (Figure 8.3). Marilyn Reardon's version (Color Plate 6A) is set parallel to the edge. Larger diamonds seem to be formed. Suzanne Lucy turned her blocks on point to visually form vertical rows or strips (Color Plate 6B).

When a Bow Tie block is set on point, the bow tie reads horizontally as in Elaine Anderson's version (Color Plate 2A). She added plain squares inbetween. If you turn a block on point, you'll need triangles around the edge to finish it off to a rectangle. In my Bow Tie version (Color Plate 9A), I set the blocks parallel to the edge, which makes the bow ties read diagonally. Added together, they form circles.

Sashing or lattice can be added between blocks (see "Joining Blocks" in Appendix). Charlene Phenney, in "Remembrance in Plaids" (Color Plate 4A), set her blocks on point and added lattice strips. She used a scrap approach when auditioning the fabric for the lattice. She also added dark intersection blocks.

Marion Ongerth also used a lattice approach to set her "Walk on the Wild Side" (Color Plate 15A). The strips vary in width, some being joined with a diagonal miter to almost suggest an Attic Window feeling.

Plain blocks can be alternated between design blocks to calm down the visual message (see "Joining Blocks" in Appendix). They provide a breather. The Quilt Lovers Group of Marin Needle Arts Guild used this approach in their "Antique Double Nine-Patch" (Color Plate 4B). By turning the blocks on point, they created an Irish Chain-type connection. See if you can find the one block that breaks this rhythm by using four rather than five nine-patches.

Joan Sextro also worked with an alternate pattern block in "Princeton Nine-Patch" (Color Plate 14A). The nine-patches, when set with the half-of-a-square triangles, produce a feeling of diagonal rows within the quilt. This is, of course, contrary to how the rows are actually sewn, which is in horizontal strips.

Susan Broenkow combined a Sawtooth Star with a

Photo 8.4.   Cranes and Stars (detail). 36" x 48".
Susan Broenkow, Pebble Beach, CA, 1988.

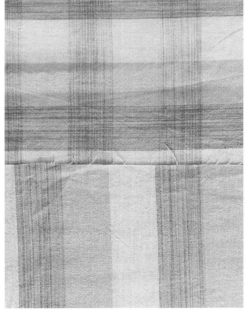

Photo 8.5.   Plaid and striped fabrics used in the Shoo Fly blocks in *Cranes and Stars* by Susan Broenkow.

Shoo Fly to make her "Cranes and Stars" (Photo 8.4). Because the Shoo Fly is done in muted beiges and grays, the blocks become very neutral; they almost read as plain blocks. What one really notices are the stars which seem to be diagonally connected. The Shoo Fly blocks also look more intricately pieced than they really are because Susan used plaid and stripe fabrics in their construction (Photo 8.5).

An Arabic Lattice block has been turned into "Plaid Lattice" by Rebecca Rohrkaste (Color Plate 8A). The design blocks are joined not corner to corner but corner to midpoint. A square (half the dimension of the block) is set into the intersection of two blocks resulting in this unusual off-set presentation. Sometimes the viewer gets the image of a horizontal-vertical lattice with four-patches at the intersections.

BORDERS

If you can find the right border, you can make almost any quilt work. That's the challenge. Sometimes a solution presents itself as you're working on the quilt, but if that doesn't happen, you don't really have to make a decision until the insides of the quilt are sewn together. Then it's actually easier to audition the possibilities because you can pin the quilt top on your design wall and slip the candidates between it and the wall; that way, you can try many different fabrics and widths. Experiment. If I'm considering using the same fabric on all sides, I find I can see the answer fastest if I compose a prospective border on two adjoining sides.

I have already mentioned several quilts that have nothing extra added on to form a border. Another example is my "Plaids on Hand" (Color Plate 9A), which structurally doesn't have a border but does visually. By darkening the perimeter units, a border is suggested. The solution came to me as I was composing the top. I thought I was almost finished making fabric combinations when I suddenly got one of those "I wonder what would happen if...?" thoughts. It meant making thirty-eight more blocks, but I liked the appearance better than the other choices I was contemplating. Oddly enough, it was harder to make the color/value choices for those outside blocks than it had been to make the choices for the other fifty blocks.

In "Plaid Lattice" (Color Plate 8A), Rebecca Rohrkaste has allowed the perimeter edges of her blocks to be the outside border, sort of like askew rick rack. This treat-

Photo 8.6.   Stars in Stripes (detail). 36" x 48". Joyce Miller, Edmonds, WA, 1989. Perimeter triangles are split to give the illusion of a continuous, dark outer border.

ment adds to the contemporary feeling of this quilt.

Joyce Miller, in her Economy Nine-Patch called "Stars in Stripes" (Color Plate 7A), seemingly extended her perimeter blocks into the border area. The visual border is actually composed of the triangles which are necessary to finish off the quilt top to a rectangle (see "Joining Blocks" in Appendix). When split into two shapes and executed with a value change, the result no longer reads as large triangles. The continuous border plaid seemingly floats under the extended on-point blocks (Photo 8.6).

Plaids make an interesting border. For a subtle contrast, Suzanne Lucy in "Angles and Squares" (Color Plate 6B) used two different plaid fabrics, similar in color and value but differing in scale. One of the plaids reads like a solid. Directionals are also useful if you end up with a quilt top that feels too busy. Remember, on-grain directionals stop the eye, so used in a border, they can calm a hectic design.

Photo 8.7.   49er Fever (detail).
78" x 78". Carolie Hensley, Walnut
Creek, CA, 1989.

Photo 8.8.   Goodbye the Nasturtiums (detail). 75" x 45".
Roberta Horton, Berkeley, CA, 1988. Plaid fabric is misaligned
when patched into the border to break down the formal feel of
the plaid used for the border.

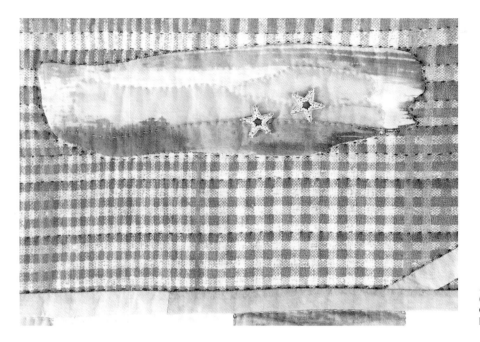

Photo 8.9.   Goodbye the Nasturtiums (detail). 75" x 45". Roberta Horton, Berkeley, CA, 1988. Star embellishments sparkle in the border area.

Carolie Hensley chose a plaid, which she set diagonally, to finish off her "49er Fever" (Photo 8.7). The interior of the Log Cabin features some plaids mixed in with the calico prints. She even managed to find some football fabric.

For "Goodbye the Nasturtiums" (Color Plate 16A), I chose a blue plaid border to represent the sky and ocean. I tried placing the plaid askew and off-setting the pattern. I found I had to line up the dark bars of the plaids to correspond with the opposite border; this felt too restricting, too formal for my informal quilt. Ultimately, I did several things to my staid plaid border. I patched the right-hand end with some misaligned wedges (Photo 8.8). It felt right to patch the old Mendocino end of the quilt. Then to further break up the border, I found I had to bisect the rest of the border with some color streaks. I also added some hand-dyed fabric in amorphous shapes, which may represent clouds. I even added some star embellishments to further suggest the glitz (Photo 8.9).

Another way to break up a border is to collage together a set of fabrics. Mata Rolston in "Pinwheel" (Color Plate 7B) has set off the collaged area from the body of the quilt with two inner borders, the light one visually being the important one. Notice how the red repeated both in the inner border and the collaged area provides a pleasing continuity.

Both my "38 Lines Zigzag" (Color Plate 1A) and Elaine Anderson's "Grandfather's Tie Collection" (Color Plate 2A) feature collaged borders, an approach that imparts a wonderful feeling of oldness to a quilt. Note that in both quilts the border treatments aren't the same on all four edges. This lessens the feel of control or structure. For example, formal medallion quilts, where control is a desirable quality, usually feature matching borders.

This compulsion for sameness is sometimes really a matter of not knowing what else to do. It's a matter of stopping our thought processes too soon. Look at Nancy Mahoney's "Flock of Geese" (Color Plate 5A).

She has an inner border on all four sides of the quilt but she used two separate patterns, a fine example of letting thought processes just go, until something new and creative turns up.

Charisa Anderson made the outside edge of "Plaids and Lines" glow with the addition of her border (Color Plate 3C). Figure 8.4 shows some simple pieced borders that can be used for the inner or outer border.

When you're ready to cut fabric for your borders, be sure to use the center middle measurement of the quilt as a guide, not the outside edge. Quilts frequently become stretched around the perimeter because of handling. Using the outside figure only continues the distortion. It's better to get back to the true measurement and ease in any fullness if necessary (Figure 8.5).

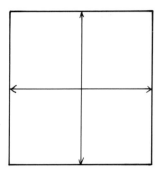

Figure 8.5.   Use the center middle measurement as a guide for border dimensions.

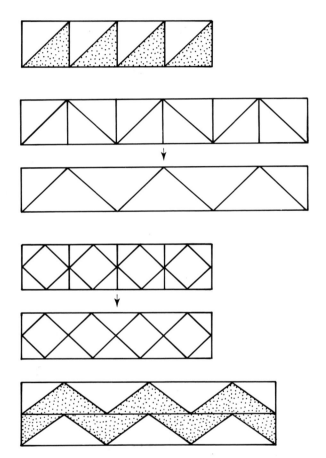

Figure 8.4.   Simple Pieced Borders

9

BACKINGS, BINDINGS, AND LABELS

How a quilt is finished says a lot about the quiltmaker. Unfortunately, many quilters don't take advantage of the creative opportunity presented by backings, bindings, and quilt labels. These areas are quite important in making a statement. In fact, viewers often carefully scrutinize them beyond their importance. Because judges must seek minute differences between quilts, backings and bindings tend to merit a very close inspection. Remember, too, given the opportunity, most quilters will turn over a corner of a quilt to see the backing selection.

BACKINGS

Backings can be thought of as a blank canvas waiting to happen. I like the back to "go" with the front, but I also want it to be a surprise, to make an additional statement. Though the easiest solution is to repeat fabric from the front of the quilt, sometimes that feels too safe unless the fabric is presented in an interesting way, perhaps cut up and reassembled.

I often place fabrics that are a new category for me on the backs of quilts. For example, I eagerly used big florals on the back of a quilt long before I let them sneak around to make a guest appearance on the front. Perhaps this process allows me time to get used to a new or more flamboyant type of fabric. In fact, I think I first became interested in directionals when I saw my sister, Mary Mashuta, use some plaid as a backing on one of her small quilts. My initial thought was that the fabric was kind of homely, but I was surprised how pleasant it looked as part of the quilt.

Early on, I was satisfied with merely a wonderful or even just an appropriate choice for my backing, but lately I've felt it necessary to collage the backs. Of course, I prefer to have the seams on the front and back staggered whenever possible. I used the fabric leftover from the front of "38 Lines Zigzag" (Color Plates 1A and 1B) to compose the pieced backing. I decided to use a format of simple squares because I felt it went along with the humble personality of the quilt, my inspiration being early quilts. When there wasn't sufficient fabric for a square, I patched it with matching fabric, if available, or something somehow related (Photo 9.1).

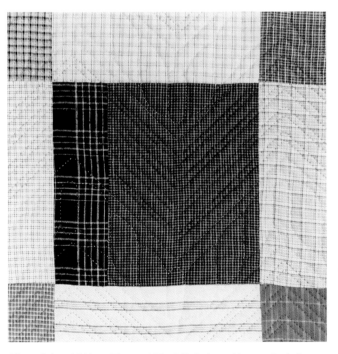

Photo 9.1. 38 Lines Zigzag. 65" x 81". Roberta Horton, Berkeley, CA, 1988. Patched block in backing of quilt.

Front

Back

Photo 9.2.   Square Within a Square. 49 1/2" x 52". Elaine Anderson,
Castro Valley, CA, 1988.

Often I crave new fabric for the back. The backing of "Plaids on Hand" (Color Plate 9A) started with the large black-and-white flowers (Color Plate 9B). The fabric seemed particularly appropriate to the flower feeling I was getting from the quilt top. (While working on the quilt top, I had often stared out my studio windows into my summer garden which was in full bloom.) After auditioning many candidates, I finally tried some fabrics hand-dyed by Debra Millard Lunn with a plaid-like design. I liked their almost blurred appearance in contrast to the hard-edge lines of the directionals used on the quilt front. Their colors also made a pleasant contrast to the black-and-white flowers. I especially liked the idea that on the front, color was in the center, while black or muted colors formed a border around the edge. The color placement reversed on the back with the black contained in a center medallion.

If you have the room, hang up the quilt top up where you can see it as you compose the backing. Keep in mind that the left edge of the quilt top will

Photo 9.4.   Plaids and Lines. 29" x 35½". Charisa Martin Anderson, Lynnwood, WA, 1988. Strip backing with a pieced insertion.

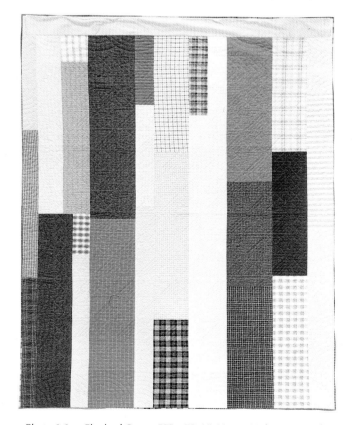

Photo 9.3.   Flock of Geese. 57" x 73½". Nancy Mahoney, Seattle, WA, 1989. Backing of the quilt is done in a hit-or-miss approach, a good way to use up leftover scraps.

match up with the right edge of the quilt back. This may require some additional thought and care since we don't normally think spatially in quite this way. When I composed the backing for "Plaids on Hand," the colors were purposely arranged to match up to the color zones on the quilt front.

Elaine Anderson, in "Square Within a Square" (Color Plate 14B), has repeated three fabrics from the front on the back of her quilt. She has, however, changed the proportions, making the plaid dominate on the back while it's merely an accent on the front. Notice the effective use of the calligraphy fabric (Photo 9.2).

Nancy Mahoney has used a hit-or-miss approach to the backing on "Flock of Geese" (Color Plate 5A). The vertical strips are a welcome contrast to the repeat block format of the front. See Photo 9.3.

Charisa Anderson's "Plaids and Lines" (Color Plate 3B) also has a strip backing, but she has used a pieced insertion to match the front borders. These half-of-a-square triangle units may well have been leftovers. Study Photo 9.4.

Photo 9.5.   Colrain Quilt (front). 82" x 82".
Colrain, MA. Collection of Ruth B. McDowell.
(Photo by David Caras.)

Photo 9.6.   Colrain Quilt. (back). 82" x 82".
Collection of Ruth B. McDowell. (Photo by David
Caras.)

Some quilts are truly two-sided. Ruth McDowell's mother found the quilt pictured in Photos 9.5 and 9.6 at a house auction in 1960. The front and backing were clearly planned to be used together because the same green and peach windowpane check is used both as the sashing on the front and as the outside border on the back. Four pieced blocks apparently leftover from the front are used to help create a giant nine-patch center for the backing which is then brought up to sufficient size by using a medallion format with borders of squares and rectangles filled with many interesting plaids and stripes. Because the quilt is tied rather than quilted, the presence of the many seams on the front and back didn't pose a construction problem.

When constructing your backing, remember to make it several inches larger, on all sides, than the quilt top. This excess can be trimmed away when the quilting is completed. If both front and back are cut the identical size, there is the chance that the backing won't stay perfectly aligned during the quilting process and may become too small in some places.

BINDINGS

I love selecting binding fabrics. Such a tiny amount shows but it's really the last chance to make a statement on the quilt front. Both the method of binding and the choice of fabric should be appropriate to the rest of the quilt. Of course, I'm advocating trying some plaids or stripes!

Fabric choice aside, a major binding decision is whether to have a bias or straight-grain binding. Believe it or not, this is one of the most controversial areas in quiltmaking today. I prefer to work with a straight-grain binding, just like the Amish, because it seems easier to me. There's not the problem of stretching inherent with bias fabric. Also straight-grain binding takes less fabric. Bias was seldom used on antique quilts because of this.

When working with a directional fabric, the design itself may influence whether you use straight grain or bias. Remember, straight lines parallel or perpendicular to the quilt edge suggest calmness while diagonal lines make for busyness. When I made "Homespun Diamond in a Square," my first plaid quilt, I intended it to be humble. I therefore chose to bind with a straight-grain plaid because it felt more plain and stark (Photo 9.7). When cutting the fabric, and later when sewing the strip on, I wasn't overly concerned if the plaid didn't remain 100% perfectly straight. It looked more appropriate to have the binding slightly off-grain here and there.

My scrap quilt "Pieced and Patched Stars" was made about the same time. Feeling it was a fancier quilt, I used plaid on the bias for the binding. This gave the edge a more decorative feeling because the message was busier (Photo 9.8).

"38 Lines Zigzag" (Color Plate 1A) is a plain quilt, but not as humble to me as "Homespun Diamond in

Photo 9.7. Homespun Diamond in a Square (detail). 71" x 61". Roberta Horton, Berkeley, CA, 1985.

Photo 9.8. Pieced and Patched Stars (detail). 48 ½" x 57 ½". Roberta Horton, Berkeley, CA, 1985.

Photo 9.9. 38 Lines Zigzag (detail). 65" x 81". Roberta Horton, Berkeley, CA, 1988.

a Square." For one thing, more fabrics were used in it. So my solution was to use straight-grain directionals but to collage them (Photo 9.9). The quilted top was pinned to my design wall, and I then composed the binding of random lengths of fabrics leftover from the backing; this "recycling" appealed to my frugal side. I knew where each piece would touch the border. I purposely left out the whites as I realized they would be too attention-getting.

Directionals pair nicely with solids and printed fabric. My "Dunn's Window" featured a solid fabric stripped

border. Placing a broken stripe perpendicular to the edge enlivened it and referred back to the prints used in the body of the quilt (Photo 9.10). My "Japanese Tea Boxes" was bordered with a large floral stripe. The plaid binding proved a pleasing contrast with the beautiful floral (Photo 9.11). This quilt, made in 1981, was the first time I had ever thought to use a directional for a binding. What a revelation! I began immediately buying plaids and stripes that might make good bindings.

The binding is applied when the quilting is completed. I like to first iron my quilt, a process much

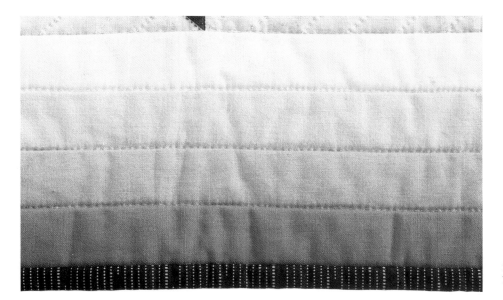

Photo 9.10. Dunn's Window (detail).
38" x 43". Roberta Horton, Berkeley, CA,
1982.

Photo 9.11. Japanese Tea Boxes (detail).
24" x 32". Roberta Horton, Berkeley, CA,
1981.

like blocking a sweater. Set the iron temperature control to "cotton" or "polyester" to correspond with the fiber content of the batting and fabric. Carefully press the quilt on the right side. I find this seems to take care of bumps and lumps and makes polyester batting look more like traditional cotton batting. Personally, I prefer the flat look of antique quilts. One final ironing reminder: make sure the sole plate of your iron is clean and that it doesn't leak dirty or rusty water.

Binding a Quilt (Figures 9.1–9.7)

1. Place pins, perpendicular to all the edges, about 1" to 2" apart (Figure 9.1).

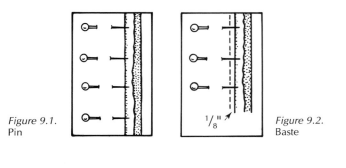

Figure 9.1.
Pin

Figure 9.2.
Baste

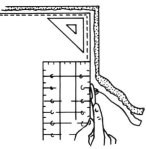

Figure 9.3.   Trim

2. Machine or hand stitch about ⅛" from the edge on all sides. Machine stitching is preferred; it really "seals" the edges (Figure 9.2).
3. Using a straight edge and rotary cutter, trim away any excess batting and backing. Check the corners with a right-angle (Figure 9.3).
4. Cut a 2" wide strip for a tight, flat binding (my preference; experiment to see if you like it wider). To determine the correct length,

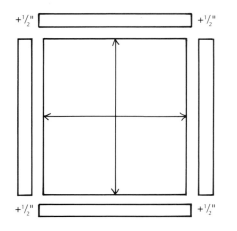

Figure 9.4.   Measure

measure across the middle of the quilt (not along the edge). Add 1" to the two shortest lengths (½" seam allowance at both ends). Many completed quilts bow or ruffle around the outside edge because unmeasured binding was merely pinned to the quilt and then cut off when it reached a corner. This can accentuate any accidental stretching that has happened in quilt construction. Using the middle-of-the-quilt measurement will get you back on track (Figure 9.4).

5. Fold the binding in half with right sides out, then press. Be very careful with bias binding not to stretch it (Figure 9.5). Pin the binding to the longest edges on the front of the quilt, starting at the corners. It helps to mark quarter and halfway points on both the quilt and binding and to connect the two at these points first (Figure 9.6). Continue to pin, easing if necessary. Any fullness will be evenly distributed. Machine stitch at ¼".

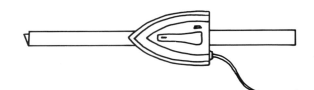

Figure 9.5.   Press Binding

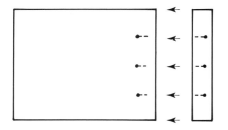

Figure 9.6.   Mark Quarter and Halfway Marks

6. Follow the same procedure for the remaining two edges. This time there will be a seam allowance at the ends (Figure 9.4 again).
7. Turn the bindings to the back side and stitch by hand. The ends with the seam allowance can be tucked under and closely stitched (Figure 9.7).

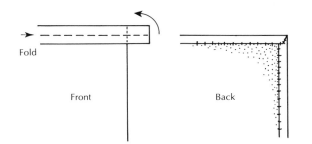

Fold

Front   Back

Figure 9.7.   Turn Binding and Stitch

LABELS

Plaids and stripes can even contribute to the signature on your quilt or to the label for the back. For example, Marion Ongerth signed her name within a striped area on the front of "Still Life with Plaids." She used a running stitch and embroidery floss (Photo 9.12).

Suzanne Lucy printed the information on her label within the confines of a striped fabric (Photo 9.13), and Charisa Anderson used a permanent pen to write her

Photo 9.12.   Still Life with Plaids (detail). 51" x 79". © Marion Ongerth, Berkeley, CA, 1989.

Photo 9.13.   Angles and Squares (detail). 49" x 61". Suzanne Lucy, Deming, WA, 1989.

holiday greetings to her mother. Notice the little plaid designs she drew on the label (Photo 9.14), and the interesting angle she used in its placement. George Taylor wrote directly onto the backing of his quilt (Photo 9.15).

Finally, when signing or labeling your quilt, make sure you heat set the writing, whether in ink or by printer. As you finish a project—especially a dramatic one featuring the successful and innovative use of plaids and stripes—you want to be sure the viewer can easily identify the creator!

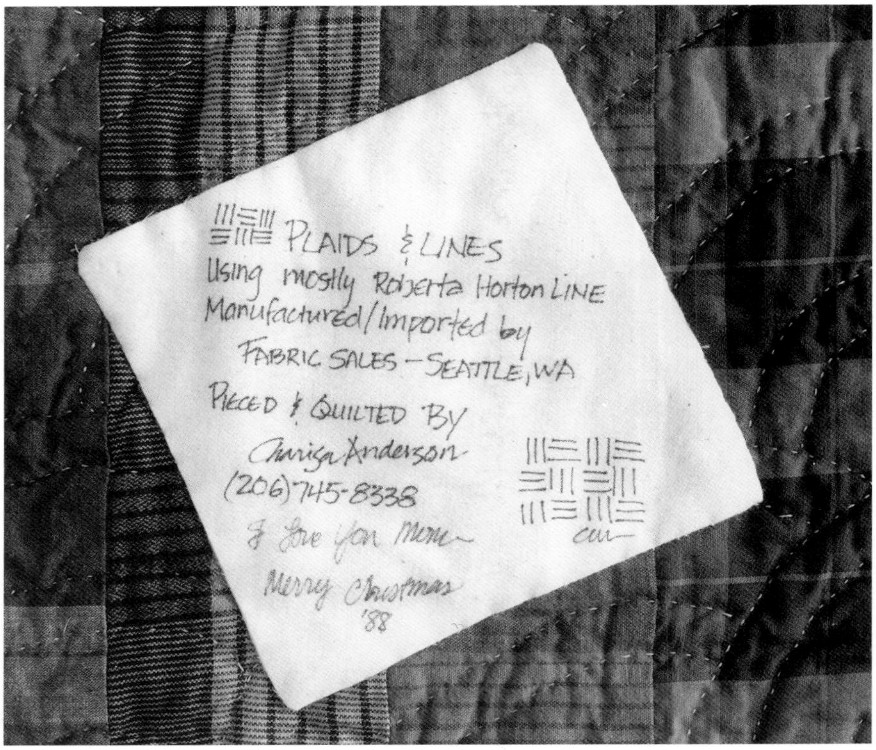

Photo 9.14.   Plaids and Lines (detail). 29" x 35 ½". Charisa Martin Anderson, Lynnwood, WA, 1988.

Photo 9.15.   Marie Pauline (detail). 38" x 65'. George Taylor, Anchorage, AK, 1989.

10

QUILTING

Directional fabrics are quite easy to quilt because it's so hard to see a quilting design on them due to their strong patterning. In other words, why bother to try a fancy design when it will be hard to mark and it won't show anyway.

But when some quilting is needed, the directional fabric itself may provide the design. Plaids, especially, are a wonderful pattern for quilting. Study the detail of my "Pieced and Patched Stars" (Photo 10.1). As you can see, quilting on the thread lines often adds a feeling of dimension. By itself, the ikat fabric used in my

Photo 10.2. *Homespun Diamond in a Square* (detail). 71" x 61". Roberta Horton, Berkeley, CA, 1985.

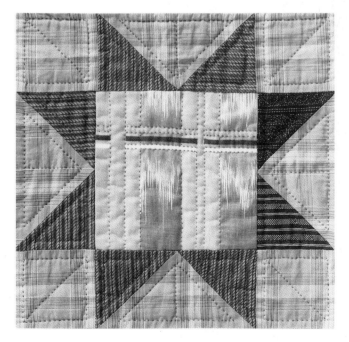

Photo 10.1. *Pieced and Patched Stars*. (detail). 48 1/2" x 57 1/2". Roberta Horton, Berkeley, CA, 1985.

"Homespun Diamond in a Square" didn't provide a strong enough suggestion for a quilting pattern, so I built a compatible triangle design over it (Photo 10.2).

When working with small, low contrast stripes, it often works well to quilt counter to the stripe itself so that the quilting pattern will show better. Parallel lines are easy to quilt, particularly if you use masking tape as a guide. Put the tape on just as you are ready to quilt the area, and remove it promptly. (To avoid a possible residue, don't leave the tape on overnight.) Parallel lines show better than a single line because the two lines create a shadow. "Takayama Harajiku" is made

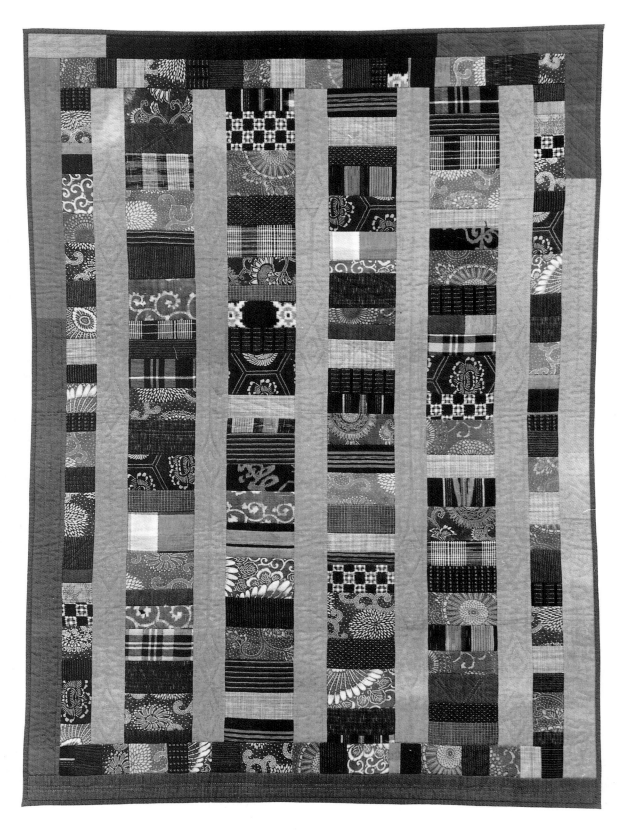

Photo 10.3.   Takayama Harajiku. 42" x 58". Roberta Horton,
Berkeley, CA, 1987.

Photo 10.4. Takayama Harajiku (detail). 42" x 58". Roberta Horton, Berkeley, CA, 1987.

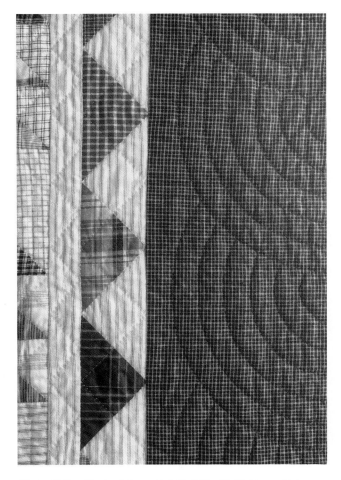

Photo 10.5. Flock of Geese (detail). 57" x 73.5". Nancy Mahoney, Seattle, WA, 1989. Quilting done with quilting thread.

from antique Japanese fabric (Photo 10.3). The florals were stitched with quilting that reflected the patterns and curved lines. The striped fabric was necessary to calm down the busyness of the high contrast florals. Quilting the stripes very simply provided a nice contrast as well. Here I felt it was necessary to bring out the calm qualities of the directionals used. Look at Photo 10.4 to see what I mean.

Parallel lines are also used in the curved fan quilting pattern. Nancy Mahoney executed a row of this pattern for her border in "Flock of Geese" (Photo 10.5). Charisa Anderson in "Plaids and Lines" (Color Plate 3B), Charlene Phenney in "Remembrance in Plaids" (Color Plate 4A), and Judy Sogn in "Hit and Miss" (Color Plate 10C) all chose to do the fans in an allover version across the surface of their quilts. Charlene and Judy used perle cotton thread instead of quilting thread for a cruder, more humble effect. See Photo 10.6.

George Taylor went several steps further in "Marie Pauline" (Color Plate 12C). He used perle cotton for the quilting, with the knots and tails left exposed rather than buried in the quilt, then added buttons as an embellishment. They were attached as part of the quilting process itself: while the quilting stitches were being taken, periodically the needle went up and down through the buttonholes of a button, then back down into the quilt, to continue with the regular stitches (Photo 10.7). The technique is unorthodox, but fun!

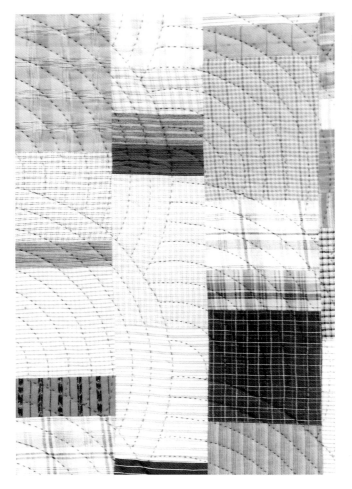

Photo 10.6.   Hit and Miss (detail). 39" x 50".
Judy Sogn, Seattle, WA, 1989.
Quilting done with perle cotton thread.

Button embellishment is better suited to a wallhanging than to a serious bed quilt which is intended to receive heavy wear.

There's a growing interest in machine quilting, and quilts made of directionals are a perfect place to practice your skills. Leslie Carabas machine quilted the space between the stripes with a curved line in "Black and White Series #7" (Photo 10.8). Marion Ongerth machine quilted with an undulating curved line to fill in the background of her blocks for "Walk on the Wild Side" (Photo 10.9).

Photo 10.7.   Marie Pauline (detail). 38" x 65". George Taylor, Anchorage, AK, 1989. Quilting done with perle cotton thread. Knots, tails, and buttons are used for embellishment.

Photo 10.8.
Black and White Series #7 (detail). 10 ½" x 12 ½".
© Leslie C. Carabas, Berkeley, CA, 1988. Quilting done by machine.

Photo 10.9.   *Walk on the Wild Side* (detail). 59" x 51".
© Marion Ongerth, Berkeley, CA, 1988. Quilting done by machine.

Photo 10.10.   38 Lines Zigzag (detail). 65" x 81".
Roberta Horton, Berkeley, CA, 1988. Fancy quilting shows best in light areas.

Cables are easy to quilt because they're created from
continuous lines; they show well because they're composed of parallel lines. The chance of a quilting pattern
showing is enhanced if it's stitched in a light value area.
I chose to place a cable in the light part of my Streak of
Lightning quilt, "38 Lines Zigzag" (Photo 10.10).

Curved parallel lines can also run across the entire
interior composition of the quilt, as in Joan Sextro's
"Princeton Nine-Patch" (Color Plate 14A). Joan felt that
a quilting pattern confined to each block would call
attention to the fact that the plaids and stripes weren't
always perfectly on-grain. An allover pattern got
around this problem. Photo 10.11 shows how she easily joined the curves from one row to another.

Besides parallel lines, enclosed areas also create a
good shadow which helps a quilting pattern to show
well. Barbara Dallas machine quilted the sashing of
"Twilight Houses" with two continuous overlapping
zigzag lines which create a diamond pattern (Photo
10.12).

Photo 10.11.   Princeton Nine-Patch (detail). 69" x 104".
Joan Sextro, Albany, CA, 1989. All-over continuous curve pattern
ignores the grainline of the directionals.

Photo 10.12.   Twilight Houses (detail).
40½" x 49". Barbara Dallas, Moraga, CA, 1989.
Two continuous overlapping zigzag lines, which
create a diamond pattern, are a good choice for
machine quilting.

CREATION OF QUILTING MOTIF

When auditioning possible quilting designs, it helps to be able to draw the shape on the quilt. As soon as I draw it, I know if I like it or not. The problem is, what to do if I don't like what I just so carefully marked on my quilt top. I prefer to draw the quilting motif on a piece of clear acetate which can be placed on the quilt where I want the design to be used. In fact, I often lay the acetate on the quilt top as I'm connecting points to form lines or fiddling with a motif. It helps to be able to clearly see both the fabric as well as the seams of the pattern. Many quilters use tissue paper to do this step, but I find that a little like seeing the quilt through a veil. The quilt top gives me so much useful information that I don't want to be denied any of the input. Figure 10.1 shows possible quilting motifs for "Plaids On Hand." My final choice is shown in Photo 10.13.

Acetate, in tablets or rolls, is available from art supply stores. It's a general purpose, clear film used for

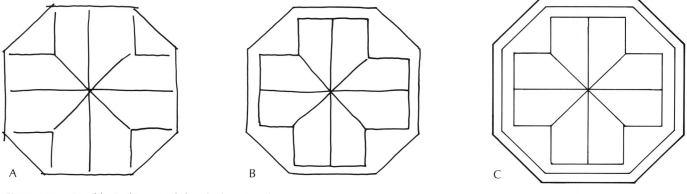

Figure 10.1.   Possible Quilting Motifs for *Plaids on Hand*

Photo 10.13.   Plaids on Hand (detail). 59" x 47".
Roberta Horton, Berkeley, CA, 1989.

overlays, color separations, and layouts. Different types of marking pens are available, each with pluses and minuses. Water-based pens require a damp cloth to remove or alter the image. Dry-erase pens are fast drying and low odor but the powder residue created when you remove the motif could get onto your quilt top. There are also fast-drying permanent markers for those of us who make irrevocable decisions. I prefer the water based-pens. After I select my design, I then transfer it to tissue, cardboard, or plastic template material for actual use.

Refer back to Chapter 6 on appliqué for help in creating motifs for quilting patterns. Information in that chapter on changing the size of a pattern may also be helpful.

I used acetate when I made some of the quilting decisions in "Goodbye the Nasturtiums" (Color Plate 16A). Shapes were quilted right at the seams but some shapes were large enough to warrant additional quilting. Figure 10.2 shows the possibilities I considered before making my final choice (Photo 10.14).

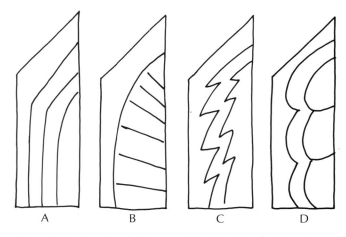

Figure 10.2. Possible Quilting Motifs for *Goodbye the Nasturtiums*

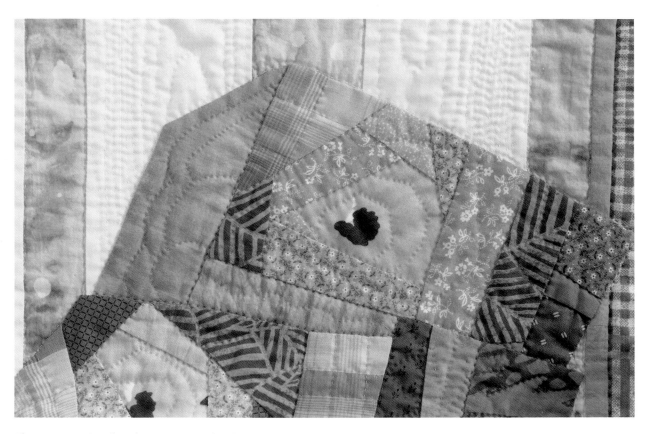

Photo 10.14. Goodbye the Nasturtiums (detail). 75" x 45". Roberta Horton, Berkeley, CA, 1988.

APPENDIX

SOURCES

The Cotton Club
P.O. Box 2263
Boise, ID 83701
208/345-5567
*Lines and Mood Indigo fabric
collections by Roberta Horton*

The Cotton Patch
Carolie Hensley
1025 Brown Avenue
Lafayette, CA 94549
415/284-1177
*Lines, Homespun Heritage II, and
Mood Indigo fabric collections by
Roberta Horton; Little Foot press-
er foot and reducing glasses*

Graves Enterprises
Lynn Graves
605 Bledsoe NW
Albuquerque, NM 87107
505/345-7647
*Little Foot presser foot (not
available for slant needle or long
shank machines at this time)*

TECHNIQUES

A. Half-of-a-square Triangles (Thanks to Barbara Johannah)

1. Determine desired size of finished triangle unit. To this always add $7/8''$ to determine X (Figure A.1).

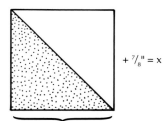

$$+ \frac{7}{8}'' = x$$

Figure A.1.

2. Draw a grid on the wrong side of one of the fabrics to be used for the triangle units. The grid should contain enough squares to equal half the number of completed units desired (Figure A.2).

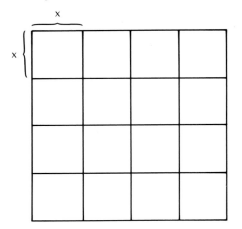

Figure A.2.

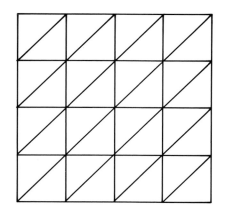

Figure A.3.

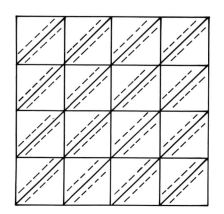

Figure A.4.

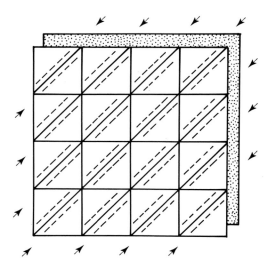

Figure A.5.

3. Draw diagonal lines across the grid (Figure A.3).
4. Add ¼" seam allowance lines (Figure A.4).
5. Position fabric with grid over second fabric to be used for triangle units, right sides together. Pin. Sew along seam allowance lines, up one seam and down the next. Skip across unmarked corners (Figure A.5).
6. Press, and cut. Press individual units (Figure A.6).

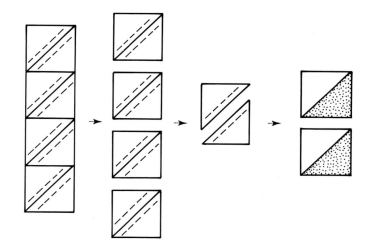

Figure A.6.

B. Joining Blocks

1. Sashing (Figure A.7)

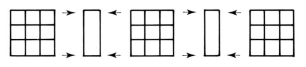

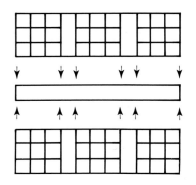

Figure A.7.

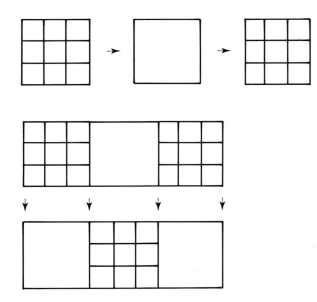

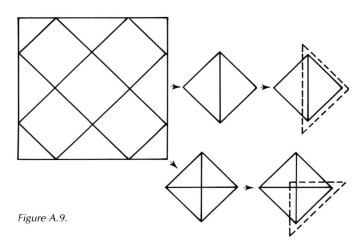

Figure A.8.

2. Alternate block (Figure A.8)
3. On point, with perimeter triangles (Figure A.9)

Figure A.9.

C. Design Wall

Ideally you should be able to place fabric cut-outs on this surface and move them around easily until your quilt design is composed. At this point, fabric pieces should be pinned into position until sewing is completed.

1. Select fabric with a slight nap that cut-out shapes will adhere to easily. Possibilities

include felt, Pellon Fleece™, Thermo Lamb™, etc.
2. Install fabric, trying to keep it taut. Here are some possible approaches (Figure A.10):
    a. tack fabric permanently to wall
    b. form a frame with artists stretcher bars; tack fabric to this and hang from wall
    c. fold under and sew a narrow pocket at top and bottom of fabric; insert rods and hang construction from top rod
3. When a permanent installation is possible, there should be provision for pinning into the design wall. This can be achieved by first attaching a bulletin-board-like surface to the wall that will accommodate pins. The fabric is then tacked over this. Check at your lumber supply store for ideas for design wall materials. Celotex, an inexpensive insulation board, is one possibility.

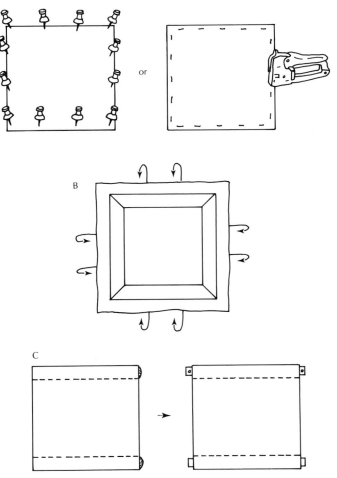

Figure A.10.

BIBLIOGRAPHY

Fanning, Robbie, and Tony Fanning. *The Complete Book of Machine Quilting*. Radnor, Pennsylvania: Chilton Book Company, 1980.

Fennelly, Catherine. *Textiles in New England, 1790–1840*. Sturbridge, Massachusetts: Old Sturbridge Village, 1961.

Haight, Ernest B. *Practical Machine-Quilting for the Homemaker*. David City, Nebraska: Ernest B. Haight, 1974.

Hargrave, Harriet. *Heirloom Machine Quilting*. Westminster, California: Burdett Publications, 1987.

Johannah, Barbara. *Continuous Curve Quilting*. Menlo Park, California: Pride of the Forest, 1980.

Leman, Bonnie, and Judy Martin. *Log Cabin Quilts*. Wheatridge, Colorado: Moon Over the Mountain Publishing Company, 1980.

Montgomery, Florence M. *Textiles in America 1650–1870*. New York: Norton, n.d.

Orlofsky, Patsy, and Myron Orlofsky. *Quilts in America*. New York: McGraw-Hill, 1974.

Penders, Mary Coyne. *Color and Cloth*. San Francisco: The Quilt Digest Press, 1989.

Walker, Sandra Rambo. *Country Cloth to Coverlets*. Lewisburg, Pennsylvania: Oral Traditions Project, 1981.

UTILITY QUILTS

Gero, Annette. "The Folklore of the Australian Wagga," in *Pieced by Mother*. Lewisburg, Pennsylvania: Oral Traditions Project, 1988.

Irwin, John Rice. *A People and Their Quilts*. Exton, Pennsylvania: Schiffer Publishing Limited, 1983.

Lasansky, Jeannette. "The Role of Haps in Central Pennsylvania's 19th and 20th Century Quiltmaking Traditions," in *Undercoverings*. Mill Valley, California: American Quilt Study Group, 1985.

McKendry, Ruth. *Quilts and Other Bed Coverings in the Canadian Tradition*. Toronto: Van Nostrand Reinhold, 1979.

Newman, Joyce Joines. "Making Do," in *North Carolina Quilts*. Chapel Hill: The University of North Carolina Press, 1988.

Pickens, Nora. *Just a Patchwork Quilt: Scrap Quilts in Early Twentieth-Century New Mexico*. Ft. Collins, Colorado: Colorado State University, 1987.

Rae, Janet. *Quilts of the British Isles*. New York: Dutton, 1987.

AFRICAN-AMERICAN QUILTS

Ferris, William. *Afro-American Folk Art and Crafts.* Jackson: University of Mississippi Press, 1983.

Ferris, William. *Local Color: A Sense of Place in Folk Art.* New York: McGraw-Hill, 1982.

Freeman, Roland. *Something to Keep You Warm.* Jackson: Mississippi Department of Archives and History, 1981.

Leon, Eli. "Cut It Down the Middle and Send It to the Other Side." *Threads Magazine*, No. 19, Oct./Nov. 1988.

Leon, Eli. *Who'd a Thought It: Improvisation in African-American Quiltmaking.* San Francisco: San Francisco Craft & Folk Art Museum, 1987.

McKinney, Nancy. *Traditions in Cloth: Afro-American Quilts/West African Textiles.* Los Angeles: California Afro-American Museum, 1986.

Picton, John, et al. *African Textiles.* London: British Museum Publications, 1979.

Price, Sally, and Richard Price. *Afro-American Arts of the Suriname Rain Forest.* Los Angeles: Museum of Cultural History, 1980.

Wahlman, Maude Southwell. "African-American Quilts: Tracing the Aesthetic Principles." *The Clarion*, Vol. 14, No. 2, Spring 1989.

Wahlman, Maude Southwell, et al. *Ten Afro-American Quilters.* Oxford: Center for the Study of Southern Culture, University of Mississippi, 1983.

ABOUT THE AUTHOR

Roberta Horton has been teaching quiltmaking since 1972, including California's first state accredited adult education course on quilts. She has taught and lectured throughout the United States as well as in Canada, Japan, New Zealand, and Australia.

Roberta authored *Stained Glass Quilting Technique*, *An Amish Adventure: A Workbook for Color in Quilts*, and *Calico and Beyond: The Use of Patterned Fabric in Quilts*. She was also the major consultant for Sunset's *Quilting*.

Roberta has designed several collections of plaids and stripes for Fabric Sales Company of Seattle. Some of the fabrics are based on the wonderful directionals found in antique quilts; others are inspired by antique Japanese textiles. The 100% cotton fabric, handwoven in India, has been used by many of the quiltmakers featured in this book.

Roberta Horton resides in Berkeley, California.

Write for a free catalog of
other fine quilting books from
C & T Publishing
P.O. Box 1456
Lafayette, CA 94549